J.T.F.

Dinner in the Garden

Heirloom Tomato Salad with Dill S...
White Peach & Pineapple Salad
Tossed Greens with Lemon Vinaigrette
Shrimp Rémoulade
& Brandied Blossom Fritters
Summer Berries with Mint
Whipped Cream

J.T.F.

Dinner on the Dock

Oysters Beaufort
Summer Squash with Feta & ... Tomat...
Peach Salad with Honey Goat Cheese
& White Balsamic Dressing
Squash & Corn Pudding
Country Sausage Dogs
with Mimi's Mustard Sauce
Peach Tart with Rosemary Crust

J.T.F.

Opening Night Dinner

Garden Tomatoes with Watermelon & Basil
Cornmeal-Crusted Okra
with Zesty Sour Cream
Goat Cheese Tartlets
Herb-Stuffed Baked Chicken
Cornmeal-Dusted Catfish
Bacon-Wrapped Beef Filets
Southern Succotash Salad
Peach Pralines

JTF
Summer Picnic

Ants on a Log
Devilish Deviled Eggs
Goat Cheese Zucchini Roll-Ups
Caprese Panzanella
Pressed Picnic Sandwich
Pasta Salad à la Pepper
Cucumber & Radish Salad
Picnic Parfaits with Granola Crumble & Berries
Mini Brown Sugar Blueberry Pies

JTF
Rehearsal Dinner
on the grounds

Baked Chicken with Peach Glaze
Spinach Salad with Berries & Feta Cheese
& Honey-Lemon Vinaigrette
Pimento Cheese Mini Sandwiches
French Green Beans
Tortellini Salad with Artichokes, Tomatoes & Ol
Cucumber Sandwiches
Gazpacho Shooters
Watermelon Ice
Sour Cream Biscuits
Orange Sorbet with Baboo's
Mama Doris's Banana Pudding wi

JTF
Family Reunion

-LUNCH-
Strawberry-Almond Spinach Salad with Poppyseed Dressing
Asian-Style Chicken Salad with Sesame Dressing
Basil-Caper Shrimp Salad
Corn & Onion Salad
Feta and Olive Pasta Salad
Potato Salad
Herb & Poppyseed Rolls
Jalapeño Corn Muffins
Peach Buttermilk Pound Cake
Chocolate-Glazed Chocolate Pound Cake
-DINNER-
Fried Chicken
Sweet-and-Sour Slaw
Gerry's World-Famous Baked Beans
Mema's Macaroni & Cheese
Deluxe Mac 'n' Cheese
with Steamer's Sauce

Dinner on the Grounds

Southern Suppers and Soirées

Dinner on the Grounds

Southern Suppers and Soirées

JAMES T. FARMER III

Photographs by EMILY FOLLOWILL *and* MAGGIE YELTON

GIBBS SMITH
TO ENRICH AND INSPIRE HUMANKIND

To my beloved grandmother, Sarah Ann Bates Granade.
In childhood I coined your name Mimi—you shaped my life.
Your life taught me to feed folks body and soul; thus, your
legacy is the highest honor for me to uphold.

First Edition
18 17 16 15 14   5 4 3 2 1

Text © 2014 James T. Farmer III
Photographs © 2014 Emily Followill, Maggie Yelton, and
Ashlee Culverhouse, as noted on page 203
Menu illustrations © 2014 Parkway Press and Maggie
Coody Griffin

Published by
Gibbs Smith
P.O. Box 667
Layton, Utah 84041

1.800.835.4993 orders
www.gibbs-smith.com

Designed by Sheryl Dickert
Page production by Melissa Dymock

Printed and bound in China
Gibbs Smith books are printed on either recycled, 100%
post-consumer waste, FSC-certified papers or on paper
produced from sustainable PEFC-certified forest/
controlled wood source. Learn more at www.pefc.org.

Library of Congress Cataloging-in-Publication Data

Farmer, James T., III.
 Dinner on the grounds : Southern suppers and soirees /
James T. Farmer
III ; photographs by Emily Followill and Maggie Yelton.
— First edition.
   pages cm
Includes index.
ISBN 978-1-4236-3628-1
1. Cooking, American—Southern style. 2. Dinners and
dining—Southern states. 3. Food habits—Southern
states. I. Title.
TX715.2.S68F368 2014
641.5975—dc23
                                        2013040211

Contents

SHALL WE GATHER?

*D*inner is a celebratory, sacred Southern meal. Thanksgiving, Christmas, New Year's, Easter and Sunday—all may be followed by "dinner." Supper is a non-celebratory evening meal, though sacred nonetheless.

"Dinner on the grounds"—we hear this colloquial saying, and memories of potlucks, covered dishes and family-and-friend gatherings wash our memories with nostalgic delight. For many Southerners, a dinner on the grounds has always been a church-wide meal associated with a homecoming service. The cardinal rule: families bring a dish that can feed their brood plus one, usually.

When I was growing up Baptist, these dishes were often casseroles or congealed salads, the epitome of Southern comfort food. But the nature of these gatherings brought about the best of Southern culinary wonders. Garden and farm-to-table foodstuffs are the Southern way; thus a dinner on the grounds provided a dichotomy that was indicative of our cooking culture. Fried chicken, ham, barbeque (that meant pork, in the Deep South), deviled eggs, biscuits, cucumbers in vinegar, corn in nearly every fashion, aspics, "fluffs," beans, peas, okra and tomatoes, white rice, brown rice, rice consommés, and red beans and rice could be found atop tables strewn under live oaks, whose branches dripping with moss further framed the bucolic country-church set-

ting that enveloped the congregation gathered around the tables.

If you were smart, as I tried to be, you would recognize casserole dishes from favorite cooks; the key was to look for labels that said "From the Kitchen of . . ." or tactfully watch the ladies placing their dishes on the table. Thus a trained eye could spot the best of the best of the smorgasbord and walk away with a bowing, seemingly groaning paper plate unable to support its load until reinforced atop the table. Being able to pile a plate full of the best meant trusting your inner knowledge and not wasting a moment to fool with a dry cake, a fruit salad of canned, out-of-season fruits, or an out-of-the-box macaroni. I once asked my Granddaddy why the tables at Cedar Creek (our little country church in Abbeville—well, Pineview, or in between Abbeville and Hawkinsville proper) were made out of concrete. He told me they were constructed so as to withstand the weather, but I knew they were fabricated to hold up the very weight of not only the food laden upon them but the serving dishes too!

Heaped on these tables were Spanish pea casseroles, poppyseed chicken casseroles, broccoli

casseroles, squash casseroles, sweet potato casseroles, veggie casseroles of all sorts, the list goes on ad infinitum! Desserts ranged from pies, cobblers and crisps boasting the fruits of the season to pound cakes, trifles, cookies, puddings and layered cakes. There would be a caramel cake, a multi-layered chocolate cake or two (usually there's a healthy rivalry within the church over whose cake-with-a-dozen-plus-thin-layers is best), coconut cake, red velvet cake and carrot cake holding court on the dessert table—each a temptation in its own right.

All this was offered from a varying fashion and array of cookware. Pyrex dishes in every shape and from every collection of the last century, tin foil pans (aluminum foil, for those above the Mason-Dixon Line), Dutch ovens, heirloom silver, disposable cartons, Corelle, iron skillets and a sundry of other vessels could be found billowing forth their offerings with Southern savoir faire.

These Sunday dinners after the worship service were times of food, fun, family and fellowship. Traditions were upheld, renewed and commenced at these dinners. Memories were relived and made simultaneously. Generations mingled together, loved ones were held dear and those who had passed on were canonized—depending on how good their pound cake was!

BEYOND THE CHURCH DINNER

This phrase "dinner on the grounds," though, has in more recent years become synonymous with gatherings and celebrations beyond the churchyard. A dinner on the grounds in Southern nomenclature has transcended into our custom of celebrating a season, a harvest, an event, a milestone or simply a happy day in the manner and style of our heritage. We gather together to feed the body and the soul. These jamborees, barbeques and get-togethers are epicenters of Southern culture and have thus expanded into an array of different venues.

A dinner on the grounds may simply be a family picnic under the oak tree in the front yard. Your grounds may be your garden, and so dinner on said grounds may be a garden party. A family reunion on the family land may be a dinner on the grounds, as can a dinner in a barn on your farm to celebrate a harvest. Your grounds may tatter into marshy water, lakeside edges, coastal channels or river bends, and dinner on the grounds may in turn be dinner on the dock. Your grounds may be the mountaintops of Appalachia and your dinner on these grounds may be set amidst the grandeur of these mountains.

Perhaps your dinner is the welcoming of a new member into the family. A baby's arrival is fêted and showered with love and anticipation and decorated with the reflections of the season. Could your dinner on the grounds be a rehearsal dinner or a reception? A wedding and all the festivities associated with it may be a dinner for hundreds of friends and families upon grounds that have hosted familial celebration for generations.

The menus for these dinners on the grounds are tailored to the event's personality, for they take on a life of their own. A host or hostess gleans from those who have hosted before them, in turn weaving their own touch into the fabric of these traditions. The food is a mirror of our connection and collection from the land and a reverence for the season. No two dinners are the same, yet they are ever so similar in their premise—a foundation of history, heritage, family ties and friendships running soulfully deep.

Southern dinners on the grounds are the culmination of people's passion for food, the drive to preserve our customs and legacies and the yearning to instill these practices in the next generation's lives. You may very well be asked in the South, "Who are your people?" I'm pleased as punch to not necessarily answer that question with upstanding surnames and maiden names and bloodlines alone, but with the confidence that comes with knowing one's heritage—an intertwined legacy and lineage of folks with a common bond.

My people, my fellow Southerners, hail from a place that values familial custom, learns from its treasured past, holds fast to the truth, revels in the simple elegance of our landscape and knows the power of gathering together for a meal. These people—my people, y'all—are the sort of folks who crave the spiritual and physical power of food, wherever it is served—but especially hungered after when dinner is served on the grounds.

WE *gather together* TO FEED
THE BODY AND THE SOUL.

Family

REUNION

JFF

Family Reunion

-LUNCH-

Strawberry-Almond Spinach Salad with Poppyseed Dressing
Asian-Style Chicken Salad with Sesame Dressing
Basil-Caper Shrimp Salad
Corn & Onion Salad
Feta and Olive Pasta Salad
Potato Salad
Herb & Poppy Seed Rolls
Jalapeno Corn Muffins
Peach Buttermilk Pound Cake
Chocolate-Glazed Chocolate Pound Cake

-DINNER-

Fried Chicken
Sweet-and-Sour Slaw
Gerry's World-Famous Baked Beans
Mema's Macaroni & Cheese
Deluxe Mac 'n' Cheese
Smoked Boston Butt with Steamer's Sauce

We gather, in gaggles of greats and grands, with aunts and uncles, parents and grandparents, siblings and cousins galore. These festivities are known as family reunions, and such events are vital to bonding with people who share our bloodlines.

Your reunion may be on an ancestral land, or perhaps a church filled with familial history and provenance. Dinners on the grounds are often thus—shared meals on some ground sacred in spirit and full of nostalgia. A potluck, a barbeque, a fish fry, or a Lowcountry boil may be as much a part of your heritage as is your genetic disposition. On my mother's side of the family, the Granades, we have gathered every few years for a reunion proper (personalized tee shirts for the event make it proper, mind you), and all the aforementioned types of meals have been at the heart of these gatherings.

Though our reunions are punctuated throughout the years with gatherings for weddings, funerals, graduations and births, we do not consider these events "family reunions." They are milestones and life celebrations to be cherished, but the preoccupation with the event's pomp and circumstance often trumps the renewal of familial bonds. Thus, it is important to gather as Granades every so often for the purpose of simply being together. We laugh, cry, rejoice, mourn, socialize, and eat— and thus feed our hearts and souls as a family.

The main day of the reunion is often a two-part feeding, beginning with a light luncheon of salads and ending with a dinner of more substance. A symphony of cool salads spread across the serving table—along with sliced 'maters, Herb and Poppyseed Rolls, Jalapeño Corn Muffins, Peanut Butter Cookies and two kinds of pound cake— start the feeding frenzy.

Later in the evening, after an afternoon of games, storytelling or maybe even a nap, the evening meal will commence, featuring some heavy hitters from the Southern culinary repertoire. Barbeque (that's pork, for us) takes center stage in the form of a smoked Boston butt lathered with Steamer's famous barbeque sauce. Fried chicken, macaroni and cheese, coleslaw, baked beans and

watermelon round out the evening menu. An assortment of cakes, cobblers, pies and ice cream keep things sweet throughout the day.

We aren't afraid to mix the good silver with plastic dishes. Serving pieces with age and legacy meld with tin foil and plastic wrap. Every hydrangea in the yard is stuffed into Mason jars, urns, vases and buckets to adorn the plaid-clad tabletops. This mix of traditional pieces, modern accouterments, garden flowers and fun linens isn't just décor; it is a representation of the mix that makes up our family. The pieces can stand on their own, but they become something much more when brought together.

The laughter of children and grownups alike, cicadas serenading in the pines, a cousin's guitar gently strummed and the motorized hum of the ice cream churn—these sounds of a reunion are the soundtrack of a Southern summer. We gather as Granades—as do y'all with your family name. We gather to relish in the fact that no one else on this earth is as close, physically or genetically, as the assemblage reunited on these grounds. Family reunions are true rejuvenations of our hearts, the hearts that pump a little bit of the same lifeblood in us all.

Strawberry-Almond Spinach Salad

Serves 8

Versions of this salad have been around for years. The texture of the spinach, the crunch of the almonds and the sweetness of the strawberries—especially when strawberries are coming in fresh from the fields in late spring and early summer—are enhanced by the creaminess of the dressing.

This recipe doubles and triples very easily, thus it is a staple dish at many large gatherings and special events. Chicken, shrimp or fish can top the salad for a light lunch or evening meal, and goat cheese, feta and blue cheese also make wonderful additions. From my family to yours, I hope you enjoy this dish!

8 cups baby spinach leaves	1 pint strawberries, sliced
1 ½ cups sliced almonds, slightly toasted and lightly salted	Poppyseed Dressing

Add the spinach, almonds and strawberries to a large serving bowl and toss.

Just before serving, pour dressing over the salad and toss. You may pass extra dressing at the table, since some like to dress the already dressed salad!

POPPYSEED DRESSING

2 tablespoons apple cider vinegar	2 teaspoons poppyseeds
2 tablespoons honey	½–1 teaspoon salt
1 tablespoon mayonnaise	½ teaspoon freshly ground black pepper
½ cup plain Greek yogurt, optional*	½ cup olive oil
2 teaspoons Dijon mustard, or 1 teaspoon dry mustard and 1 teaspoon Dijon	

In a lidded jar, combine all the ingredients, except the oil, and shake. Slowly pour the olive oil into the jar and shake again. (The dressing may separate but the mustard helps act as an emulsifier.) This dressing stores for several days in the refrigerator.

The yogurt makes a creamier dressing.

Asian-Style Chicken Salad with Sesame Dressing

Serves 4–6

Lighter in calories but not light on flavor, this cool salad is a perfect meal, especially when it's hot outside. The mélange of textures and tastes have me craving this salad quite often.

1½ pounds (about 3–4) boneless skinless chicken breasts	3 stalks celery, sliced on the diagonal
Salt and pepper	1 large red pepper, ribs and seeds removed, thinly sliced
Sesame Dressing	1–2 cups bean sprouts
½ pound snow peas, cut diagonally into 2–3 pieces	1 head Chinese cabbage, julienned, optional
1–2 cups matchstick carrots	¾ cup toasted sesame seeds
3 cups sliced broccoli florets	

Brush chicken breasts with olive oil; sprinkle with salt and pepper. Roast for 30 minutes, or until cooked through but not dry. Alternatively, cook on a grill over medium heat. (If grilling, be aware that the oil will smoke up the barbeque.) Let chicken cool enough to handle, then slice thinly across the grain. Toss with ¼ cup Sesame Dressing and refrigerate until ready to use, as long as overnight.

Blanch peas, carrots, broccoli, celery and peppers in generously salted boiling water for 30 seconds. Drain and plunge into an ice water bath to stop the cooking. Drain and spread on paper towels to finish drying.

Mix chicken, blanched veggies and bean sprouts with enough dressing to coat. Arrange on a bed of julienned cabbage, if desired. Sprinkle with sesame seeds and serve.

SESAME DRESSING

1 teaspoon freshly minced ginger	1 teaspoon toasted sesame seeds
1 tablespoon toasted sesame oil	Salt and pepper
⅓ cup seasoned rice wine vinegar	1 cup canola oil
1 teaspoon sugar	

In a lidded jar or blender, shake or blend all the ingredients together, adding oil slowly if blending. I use a jar for just about all my dressings and simply shake well and then dress the salad.

Farmer's Note: I use this dressing as a marinade for fish and shrimp, too.

Basil-Caper Shrimp Salad

Serves 4

Shrimp salad is second only to chicken salad in its diverse array of preparations in the South. This version is a variation on my Sea Island Shrimp Salad—amped up with the summertime goodness of basil and the vinegary bite of capers.

1½   pounds cooked shrimp, peeled and deveined, tails on

1¾   cups apple cider vinegar

½   cup olive oil

2   lemons, sliced (squeeze juice from smaller end pieces)

1   3.75-ounce bottle of capers, with liquid

1   large Vidalia or other sweet onion, julienned

1   heaping cup basil leaves, cut in chiffonade or chopped (plus more for garnish)

Salt and freshly ground black pepper

Pat the shrimp dry with paper towels.

In a medium-size bowl, mix together the vinegar, oil, lemon juice, capers with liquid, onion and basil leaves. Add salt and pepper to taste.

Add the shrimp to the marinade and refrigerate for several hours, stirring a few times. When ready to serve, garnish with additional basil.

Farmer's Note: Roasting, quickly grilling, or sautéing raw shrimp wakes this dish up, too.

Corn and Onion Salad

Serves 4

Corn and onions were meant to go together. Raw or cooked, their flavors complement one another terrifically. So do their colors! This salad is scrumptious immediately upon being made or even after it sits for a spell. It is also adaptable: it may be served as a side at a picnic or reunion, as a topping for a bed of greens or pasta or even as a condiment to tacos.

5 ears sweet corn (such as Silver Queen, or your favorite variety)

½ cup diced red onion

3 tablespoons cider vinegar

3 tablespoons good-quality olive oil

½ teaspoon kosher salt

½ teaspoon freshly ground black pepper

½ cup chiffonade of fresh basil leaves

In a large pot of boiling, salted water, cook the corn for 3 minutes. Drain the water and immerse the corn in ice water to stop the cooking and set the color. When the corn is cool, cut the kernels from the cob.

Toss the kernels in a large bowl with the red onion, vinegar, olive oil, salt and pepper. Just before serving, toss in the fresh basil. Taste and adjust seasonings if needed. Serve cold.

Farmer's Note: I love corn in just about anything! An especially good ear of corn is perfectly flavorful without any cooking at all. Try mixing in some uncooked corn with the blanched corn for added texture and crispness.

Feta and Olive Pasta Salad

Serves 4–6

Need to feed an army? This salad is so simple that it can easily be doubled or tripled and made ahead of time!

1	pound rotini pasta, cooked until al dente
2	(7-ounce) packets Good Season's Italian or Zesty Italian dressing mix
1	(14-ounce) can artichoke hearts in water, well drained and blotted dry

½	cup sliced green olives with pimento, drained
½	cup sliced black olives, drained
½	cup sun-dried tomatoes (not oil-packed), diced
¾	cup crumbled feta cheese

Drain pasta, then rinse in cold water and drain again.

Mix dressing according to package directions, except use half the vinegar, water and oil called for.

In a bowl, toss the pasta, dressing, and all other ingredients to mix. Cover and refrigerate several hours or overnight. Mix well before serving. If the salad seems dry, dress with an additional mixture of Good Season's dressing.

Herb and Poppyseed Rolls

Potato Salad

Serves 4–6

Sara Jo, my sweet friend and cook extraordinaire, makes this for her deli customers and my family too. If jalapeños or other garden peppers are coming in, they make flavorful additions, as do pickled banana peppers. This is a building block potato salad: you may build upon it as you wish. Relishes, pickles and even slices of barbecue can be added to or topped onto this salad.

3	pounds red-skin potatoes		Salt and pepper
1	bunch green onions, thinly sliced	½	cup sour cream
1	large red or green bell pepper, diced	½	cup mayonnaise

Cook potatoes in salted water until very tender. Drain and let cool enough to handle. Break into large pieces using your hands or a fork. Place potatoes in a large bowl with the onions and pepper; season to taste with salt and pepper.

In a small bowl, stir together the sour cream and mayonnaise; then fold the mayonnaise mixture into the vegetables until potatoes are coated.

Herb and Poppyseed Rolls

Makes 24

Bake plenty. These go fast!

24 frozen uncooked rolls or partially cooked bakery rolls	1 heaping tablespoon each:
About 1 cup melted butter	Poppyseeds
	Fennel seeds
	Sesame seeds
	Caraway seeds

Bake rolls according to package directions. Brush with melted butter upon removing from the oven, then immediately sprinkle with seeds of your choice.

Farmer's Note: Store-bought rolls work just fine for this recipe, so use your favorite variety.

Jalapeño Corn Muffins

Makes a farmer's dozen

I am embarrassed to even begin to count how many Sea Island corn muffins I have consumed over the years. I'm surprised I could even walk out onto the beach without being mistaken for a whale! To me, the Sea Island corn muffin is, bar none, the best corn muffin. Adding this touch of heat is simply gilding the lily. Well, serving with honey butter may be the ultimate gilding!

This is the Sea Island recipe for corn muffins. For those who have partaken of the glory that is a Sea Island corn muffin, you know that an improvement is hardly attainable, but the little jalapeño kick I've added is deliciously delightful!

1⅓	cups sugar	½	cup vegetable oil
1½	teaspoons salt	⅔	cup water
2½	cups bread flour	1	cup cream-style corn
1½	tablespoons baking powder	½–¾	cup chopped fresh seeded jalapeño
1	cup corn meal	½	cup bacon pieces
2	eggs	1	cup shredded cheddar cheese
2	tablespoons milk		

Preheat the oven to 375 degrees.

Combine the sugar, salt, flour, baking powder and corn meal together. In a separate bowl, combine the eggs, milk, oil and water and then slowly add to the dry ingredients. Scrape the bowl after adding all of the liquid and mix again to make sure there are no clumps. Stir in the cream corn and jalapeños. Fold in the bacon, and cheese.

Bake in muffin pans until a toothpick comes out clean, about 15 minutes.

Serve muffins warm or at room temperature with honey butter. Sinfully good, y'all!

HONEY BUTTER

4 ounces (1 stick) butter, room temperature	¼	cup honey

Mix butter and honey together thoroughly and put into a small serving bowl.

Peach Buttermilk Pound Cake

Serves 8–12, depending on slice width and if I'm having seconds or thirds

I adore this cake. The base itself is a classically delicious cake with hardly a parallel. Seasonal additions such as peaches are marvelous. Blueberries, blackberries, strawberries, pumpkin puree, pecans, pears and apples all meld well. For this Georgia boy, peaches are my favorite.

8   ounces (2 sticks) unsalted butter, room temperature, plus more for the pan

3   cups granulated sugar

6   large eggs plus 1 egg yolk

2–3 tablespoons vanilla extract

Finely grated lemon zest, optional (not needed if peaches are tart)

3   cups all-purpose flour

½   teaspoon baking soda

¼   teaspoon salt

1   cup buttermilk

3–4 peaches, peeled and chopped (the firmer the peach, the better they hold up in the cake, but a soft peach practically dissolves and gives a bit more flavor—baker's choice!)

Preheat the oven to 325 degrees. Lightly butter a tube or Bundt pan and place it on a baking sheet; set aside.

Using a mixer on medium speed, beat the butter and sugar together until light and fluffy. Add the eggs and egg yolk one at a time, beating after each addition. Add the vanilla and lemon zest, if using.

Whisk the flour, baking soda and salt together in a bowl. Beat the flour mixture into the butter mixture in three additions, alternating with the buttermilk, scraping down the bowl as needed. Pour the batter into the prepared pan and top with the peaches.

Bake about 1 hour and 30 minutes, or until the cake pulls away from the sides of the pan and a toothpick inserted in the middle comes out clean. Let cool on the baking sheet for 5 minutes, then transfer the pan to a rack and cool completely. Run a knife along the sides of the pan to loosen and then turn out onto a cake plate. I usually flip the cake again so the side that was the top in the oven is, once again, the top side.

Chocolate-Glazed Chocolate Pound Cake

Serves 8–12

A very traditional pound cake recipe spiked with chocolate and coffee, this Chocolate Pound Cake is easy to prepare. In my opinion, the only thing better than a good ol' pound cake is a good ol' chocolate pound cake—with chocolate ganache, of course!

8 ounces (2 sticks) unsalted butter, softened	½ teaspoon baking powder
1 cup sugar	¾ cup cocoa powder
6 large eggs, room temperature	2 tablespoons hot coffee or espresso, or 1 teaspoon instant coffee or espresso
1½ cups all-purpose flour	

Preheat the oven to 350 degrees. Lightly butter a Bundt pan or an 8-inch tube pan and line it with parchment paper, leaving a slight overhang as handles.*

Using a stand mixer or electric hand mixer, beat the butter and sugar until light and creamy. Add the eggs one at a time and beat well after each addition.

Sift the flour, baking powder and cocoa over the butter mixture and mix on low speed until combined. Taste the batter; add the coffee and mix on low speed and then taste the batter again to see how the chocolate flavor has been intensified.

Spoon the mixture into prepared pan and smooth the batter with an offset spatula. Bake for 1 hour (start checking at 40 minutes), or until the cake pulls away from the sides of the pan and a toothpick inserted in the middle comes out clean. Cool on a wire rack for 10 minutes. Then, using the sides of the parchment paper, gently lift the cake out of the pan to finish cooling.

*If using a Bundt ban with recesses or a pattern, there's no need to use the parchment paper. I mainly use it when baking in a smooth-sided tube pan.

FOR THE GANACHE:

1½ cups chopped dark chocolate

1½ cups heavy whipping cream

Place the chopped chocolate in a medium-size bowl. In a heavy-bottomed saucepan, warm the whipping cream over low heat. **Caution:** Do not let the cream come to a boil.

Pour the warmed cream over the chocolate and allow the cream and chocolate to sit, undisturbed, for 3 to 5 minutes. Gently fold and then stir the two ingredients until all the chocolate is melted and completely blended into a smooth ganache.

Set your cooled cake on a rack with a pan below to catch the drippings—these are too good to waste! When the ganache is close to room temperature but still slightly warm, begin spooning, or even pouring, it over the cooled pound cake.

Fried Chicken

Serves 8–10

Frying chicken, in the South, is an art form that deserves the highest respect. Mimi and Mrs. Mary would whip out a skillet or a deep fryer in a heartbeat and fry all day long. Their hallmark was a heavy hand with the paprika and seasoned salt. I can fry chicken too, but if I'm entertaining a large crowd at home, Skipper John's is, bar none, the best for feeding a posse, gaggle or group in my neck of the woods.

Another maven of high praise in the world of southern cooking was Mrs. S.R. Dull. Her little blue book was first published in 1928; it taught, guided and inspired generations of Southern cooks. A classic never becomes unstylish, and this book—with its classically Southern outlook on cooking—has withstood the test of time. Some verbiage here and there may be antiquated, and some cookery or practices may be as well, but the recipes, instructions and culinary combinations are spot-on for today and our noteworthy attempt of garden- and farm-to-table eating. Following are her directions with my additions.

"Select a young chicken from 1½–2 lbs. Dress and disjoint, chill. When ready, have a deep fry pan with grease at least two inches deep. [Be sure to have some extra oil, lard or Crisco in case your oil depth is reduced during frying. Also, a lidded Dutch oven or lidded deep enameled cast-iron pan is fabulous for frying—Lodge, Le Creuset, Staub and the like.]

Sift enough flour in which to roll the chicken pieces (a cup and a half or two cups). Add salt and pepper to the flour, roll each piece in the flour and place in the hot grease. [I like to add a bit of Nature's Seasons or garlic powder, cayenne, seasoned salt or even a bit of dried bay leaf in my "dry," or flour.] *Put the largest pieces in first and on the hottest part of the pan.* [Don't crowd the pan, though. Each addition changes the temperature a bit, but only slightly. The main reason not to crowd the pan is to ensure proper browning on all sides.] *When all is in, cover for 5 minutes. Remove top and turn when the underside is well browned. Replace top for another 5 minutes, remove and cook in open pan until the side is well browned. About 30 minutes in all will be required for cooking chicken if it is not too large. Do not turn chicken but once; too much turning and too long cooking will destroy the fine flavor which is there when well cooked.*

I could not agree more, Mrs. Dull!

The fat should be deep enough to cover the pieces when it boils up."

TO MAKE CREAM:

Cream gravy is a Southern delicacy. Gravy may be ladled or poured over many things, but not fried chicken—at least in SOWEGA (Southwest Georgia.) It is totally fine, however, if some of your fried chicken soaks or "sops" up some of the gravy that cascades down from a side dish.

Brown, tomato and sawmill gravies all work well with fried chicken sides such as rice, mashed potatoes and biscuits. This is a sawmill-style gravy and can be doused with black pepper if desired. Add crumbled sausage for breakfast-style gravy!

"Pour off the grease, leaving 2 to 3 tablespoons in the pan with the browned crumbs. Add 2 tablespoons butter, 4 tablespoons flour, blend and cook until golden brown; add 1 cup milk and 1 cup hot water. Stir until smooth and the right thickness and add salt and black pepper. Pour into a gravy boat and serve with hot biscuit or dry rice. Never pour gravy over fried chicken if you wish Georgia fried chicken."

Sweet-and-Sour Slaw

Serves 4–6

A variation on my Wedding Coleslaw from *A Time to Cook,* this is a classic Southern recipe that has become a family favorite for barbeques and other dinners on the grounds. I can't resist the textural temptation of crisp cabbage and the toasty ramen noodles with vinegary, soft onions.

1 large cabbage (or mix white and purple cabbage)	1 tablespoon salt
1 small yellow bell pepper, finely chopped	1 teaspoon dry mustard
1 heaping cup shredded carrots	1 teaspoon celery seed
¾–1 cup sugar	¾ cup salad oil
1 cup apple cider vinegar	2 packages ramen noodles, broken up and lightly toasted, or 2 cups chow mein noodles, toasted
2 medium onions, minced (I like 1 Vidalia and 1 red onion)	

Chop the cabbage or slice into ribbons and mix with the pepper and carrots.

In a medium pan over medium heat, dissolve the sugar in the vinegar; add the onion, salt, mustard and celery seed.

In a lidded jar, shake and incorporate the vinegar mixture with the oil. Pour dressing over vegetables and top with toasted noodles before serving.

Farmer's Note: You may serve the slaw right away or chill it. The slaw holds up quite well when made a day ahead. Top with the noodles just before serving, though.

Uncle Gerry's World-Famous Baked Beans

Serves 6–8

Uncle Gerry's baked beans are legendary in our family and around town. He takes pride in preparing this dish for just about any event. I have a feeling he is withholding a secret ingredient or two, but he assured me this recipe would give you a good batch of baked beans nonetheless.

Every family needs an Uncle Gerry. His steady, laid-back demeanor is a good contrast to our family's lively, playful nature. I hardly know another in-law that will host and make gallons of baked beans for his wife's family reunion! Thank you, Unc!

2 (16-ounce) cans store-bought baked beans

1 (16-ounce) can black beans

1 (16-ounce) can dark red kidney beans

1 cup ketchup

2 tablespoons yellow mustard

¾ cup brown sugar

1 tablespoon liquid smoke

½ cup sweet barbeque sauce of your choosing

1 medium Vidalia onion, chopped

8–10 strips bacon

Preheat oven to 350 degrees.

Mix all the ingredients together except bacon. Pour into a large baking dish or casserole and cover with bacon slices. Bake for 1 hour, until the beans are bubbly and the bacon is crispy.

Mema's Macaroni and Cheese

Serves 10

Mema was my great-grandmother. Mimi was my grandmother. Mama is my mama. Southern maternal nomenclature runs a wide range. However, for my family, an alliterative collection of Mema, Mimi and Mama works just fine. An amazing fact about this triumvirate of women is that they all shared the same birthday—three generations of mothers and daughters!

Mema made the best macaroni and cheese. It's actually more of a macaroni custard. In fact, her recipe even says "until custard is set" in the directions. This recipe is a very Southern-style mac 'n' cheese; recipes of similar instruction can be found in dozens of old spiral-bound cookbooks across the South.

No family reunion, dinner on the grounds or major holiday is complete without a macaroni and cheese dish. This is my family's version, and I've included the deluxe version as well (facing).

1 pound elbow macaroni	Freshly ground pepper
4 ounces (1 stick) butter, sliced into pats	4 large eggs, beaten
1 pound freshly grated sharp cheddar cheese	1 cup whole milk
1 teaspoon salt	½ cup heavy whipping cream

Preheat the oven to 350 degrees.

Cook macaroni according to package directions until just slightly undercooked, no more than al dente. Drain pasta.

In a large casserole dish, make two layers of the macaroni, pats of butter, cheese, and salt and pepper to taste (I like lots of pepper, but M, M and M did/do not; so a couple pans were usually made). Recipe will make two layers.

In a medium-size mixing bowl, combine the eggs, milk and cream. Pour this mixture over casserole layers. Bake for 45 minutes to 1 hour, or until the custard is set.

Farmer's Note: This dish can be prepped the day before and cooked just before serving.

Deluxe Mac 'n' Cheese

Serves 6–8

Deluxe Macaroni 'n' Cheese is nearly nirvana, for this version takes a delicacy of Southern cuisine to a higher state of being. I feel guilty about "improving" upon my great-grandmother's recipe, but I have a selfish agenda for it. My mama makes a delicious spaghetti pie with a similar filling and I started thinking—a dangerous pastime, mind you—about how that pie filling would be an amazing addition to mac 'n' cheese. It *is* an amazing addition. I can imagine Mema now, saying, "Honey, you did such a good job. My version is better, but this is good too," as she takes her second helping.

½ pound elbow macaroni pasta

2 ounces (½ stick) butter

1 cup panko

2 cups small curd cottage cheese

1 cup sour cream

½ cup freshly grated Parmesan cheese

1 large egg, beaten

Salt and freshly ground black pepper

1 cup freshly grated sharp cheddar cheese

1 cup freshly grated white cheddar cheese

½ cup Pepper Jack cheese

Paprika

Lightly grease a square 9 x 9-inch baking dish or a 2-quart or larger casserole dish.

Cook the pasta according to package directions until al dente. Drain and set aside.

In a small bowl, melt the butter; mix it with the panko and set aside.

Preheat the oven to 350 degrees.

Combine the cottage cheese, sour cream, Parmesan cheese, egg, and salt and pepper to taste. Add the three remaining cheeses and incorporate well. Stir in the macaroni.

Turn the pasta and cheese mixture into prepared baking dish and top with the buttered panko and paprika. Bake for 45 minutes.

Farmer's Note: Ricotta cheese works lavishly well in the dish too. Adding ½ to ¾ cup is luscious! You may decrease the amount of cottage cheese in this case.

Smoked Boston Butt with Steamer's Sauce

Serves 10

Barbeque in the Deep South means pork—smoked pork, usually a Boston butt. This cut of pork derives its name from, ironically, not the lower end of the pig but the higher—more specifically, the shoulder. Historically, the style of butchery common around Boston in the 1800s and later included the shoulder bone of the hog. These shoulders were then packed into "butts," or barrels, for shipping and transport. The term *Boston butt* thus became synonymous with a pork shoulder.

8–12   pound Boston butt

Seasonings of choice

Salt and pepper

Pat the Boston butt dry with paper towels. Season meat to taste. This may include an array of spices, rubs and herbs or simply salt and pepper. Regardless of what seasonings are used, the smoke and natural flavor of this cut are the magical and delicious bits.

Wrap your seasoned shoulder in tin foil and smoke (in a smoker, grill, barbeque pit, fire pit, or oven) at a low 200- to 250-degree heat for about 8 to 12 hours, depending on the size and weight of the pork. I use the formula 1½ hours per pound at 225 degrees.

Once the meat is sufficiently cooked, (pink smoke rings have developed and the internal temperature of the meat is about 190–205 degrees), the pork may literally be pulled away from the bone and doused or dipped in barbeque sauce.

STEAMER'S SAUCE

Makes about 3 pints

There are sauces that are good and sauces that make a meal. Then there are sauces that change the way you eat. Steamer's sauce did that for me.

I cannot even begin to take any credit for this sauce. All credit is due to Mr. Steve Jenkins, aka Steamer, who was the father of my dear friend Maggie Lunsford and beloved husband of Mama J, Mrs. Melody Jenkins. Since I collect Maggies (I have a sister and a best friend named Maggie), the good Lord knew I needed a Maggie in town when the other two married and moved away. Enter Maggie Lunsford—also known as Perry Maggie.

When Maggie brought this auburn-hued, tangy sauce to dinner, we opened the jar just for a taste; my entire dinner party commenced dipping everything we could into this concoction. We dipped bread, pork and chicken and even our fingers into the Mason jar of sauce and clamored over who would be the first to pour it over a plate of pulled pork and smoked chicken. Since I've begged Perry Maggie to bring the sauce to every barbeque since then, she and Mama J finally caved in to my pleading and gave me the recipe. Says Maggie, "This is basically a guideline. You can add or take away according to your preference."

1 pint of store-brand white or apple cider vinegar (the store brand usually has less sugar)

1 medium-size jar (about 12 ounces) yellow mustard

1 (24-ounce) bottle ketchup

2 tablespoons liquid smoke

1–2 teaspoons lemon juice concentrate

Texas Pete hot sauce (play with the amount to determine spiciness)

1 medium yellow onion, chopped

Salt and pepper

In a large saucepan, simmer all ingredients for approximately 1 hour. Tinker with the flavor as desired. According to Steamer, "If your cheeks twinge, then the sauce is ready." Maggie clarifies, "The way you know it's ready is when you dip white bread into the sauce for a taste and it makes your jaws twitch. If the *smell* makes your jaw twitch, too, then it is ready."

Dinner
IN THE Garden

Dinner in the Garden

Heirloom Tomato Salad with Dill Sauce

White Peach & Pineapple Salad

Shrimp Rémoulade

Tossed Greens with Lemon Vinaigrette

& Brandied Blossom Fritters

Summer Berries with Mint

Whipped Cream

I find myself entertaining more and more outdoors rather than indoors—especially when the garden is full of blossoms, scents and textures as delectable as the menu. Mimi always said, "We eat with our eyes first." Thus, feasting visually in the garden is a fantastic appetizer to any meal.

The porch is where home and garden meet, making it an ideal setting for an outdoor dinner. A table setting is grand in a venue where hydrangeas, ferns, lush summer greenery, scents from herbs and magnolias, blooming flowers and landscape architecture abound. Playing off the porch's hybrid nature of being out of doors yet still under cover is a true design inspiration. Mixing silver with garden greenery, china and glassware with rustic tabletops, and using linens in proximity to dirt is the ultimate, fun balance of outdoor entertaining.

A place mat made of hydrangea leaves topped with heirloom dinnerware; antique jars filled with blossoms and foliage; silver containers billowing with hydrangeas; garden bits as garnish and flavors are all a part of this dinner in the garden. The menu reflects the setting and season: Heirloom Tomato Salad with Dill Sauce, Peach and Pineapple Salad, Shrimp Rémoulade, Garden Greens with Herb Vinaigrette and Brandied Blossom Fritters, and Summer Berries with Mint Whipped Cream round out this spread. The colors and hues even speak of the season with their warmth and depth. Corals, pinks, soft reds, peachy tones and greens are a part of the visual and culinary experience.

The garden is never the same from one day to the next. Blossoms bloom and fade. Foliage unfurls and progresses through the seasons. Branches become limbs, stalks become trunks and seedlings become hedges. The garden is in a state of evolution each and every day, metamorphosing with every passing minute. A dinner in this enchanting place is a delight of the highest order. There is something nearly symbolic about dining amid the grounds where many of your flavors and foods were grown.

I take such events as an evening to treasure—a dinner in the garden is a memory for a lifetime. Dinner in the garden may be a continuation of established al fresco dining habits or it may be a new tradition for you. The grounds—the garden itself—provide a harvest of sustenance and social amusement. May we eat with our eyes first and feed all of our senses during dinner in the garden. It is a time where we may gather with friends and family, serve them the season's best offerings and cherish the bounty of not only the land but also our relationships. Enjoy, y'all!

Heirloom Tomato Salad with Dill Sauce

Serves 6–8

½ cup sour cream	½ teaspoon dried dill weed
¼ cup mayonnaise	¼ teaspoon salt
2 tablespoons vinegar	½ teaspoon sugar
2 tablespoons salad oil	5-6 vine-ripened garden tomatoes
2 tablespoons grated onion	

Mix together all ingredients except tomatoes.

Peel (if desired) and quarter tomatoes. Add to the sour cream mixture and marinate all day.

Alternatively, slice the 'maters and serve with sauce drizzled over them.

White Peach and Pineapple Salad

Serves 12

Aspics, fluffs, and Jell-O salads are culinary cornerstones of the South. No Southern supper, soirée or luncheon is complete without a gelatinous dish. This dish is my ode to gelatin.

Some folks have steered away from using gelatin-laced dishes, but it's dishes like this that my Mimi and her generation loved. This particular salad is a common thread running through Mimi's childhood in Bainbridge and mine in Hawkinsville and Perry. Nearly every spiral-bound church or ladies group cookbook has a version, and this dish has been served from many a Southerner's sideboard.

I prepare and serve this salad just as Mimi did and just as her Big Mama did. I did not know her grandparents but feel connected nonetheless. The gelatin, like our bloodline, binds many generations. If bound only in a bizarre suspension of Jell-O, we Southerners are bound nevertheless. We can't fight it—genetics or gelatin.

2	small (8-ounce) cans crushed pineapple packed in juice	½	package Knox gelatin
2	small (10.75-ounce) cans mandarin oranges packed in juice	2	(3-ounce) boxes peach Jell-O
		5–6	white peaches, peeled and sliced*

Ever so slightly grease individual molds or a 9 x 13-inch rectangular container.

Drain the pineapple and oranges, reserving the juice. Add enough water to the combined juices to make 4 cups. Dissolve gelatin in ¼ cup of the juice. Boil remaining juice and add Jell-O and gelatin; stir to dissolve. When Jell-O is completely dissolved, add the fruit and stir. Pour into prepared container(s) and refrigerate until set.

To serve, unmold the salads or cut the rectangular salad into squares. Serve on a lettuce or hydrangea leaf, of course; no need to disappoint our grandmothers!

Farmer's Note: Yellow peaches will do just fine, but when white peaches are in season, they make the best salad!

Shrimp Rémoulade

Serves 12–14

This dish allows me to tell a story on my mother. When I was a young boy, Mama had a decorator from Atlanta come down and give her some ideas for our farmhouse. When you are a country mouse, a city mouse—especially a decorator from Atlanta—has supreme authority when it comes to proper interior design or architecture. Mama told this well-dressed, European-car-driving decorator that she *loved* "Carl." "Carl makes me happy. Carl makes me smile. Carl simply lights up my life," she said.

"Well, who is this 'Carl' you speak of, ma'am? Your husband is Ted!" the designer responded.

Soon thereafter, our living room was painted in Mama's favorite color—also known as "coral." From the shrimp to the sauce, this Shrimp Rémoulade is a perfect array of "Carl" hues.

½	cup tarragon vinegar		1	clove garlic, minced
2–3	tablespoons tomato ketchup		1	cup salad oil
3–4	tablespoons horseradish mustard		½	cup minced green onions, with tops
2	tablespoons grainy mustard		½	cup minced celery
2	tablespoons Dijon mustard		4	pounds medium-to-large shrimp, cleaned and cooked (boiled, baked or grilled)
1	tablespoon paprika			
1	teaspoon salt		¼	head lettuce, shredded
½	teaspoon cayenne pepper			

Mix vinegar, ketchup, mustards, paprika, salt, cayenne pepper and garlic in a small bowl. Gradually whisk in the oil. Stir in onions and celery.

Pour sauce over shrimp and marinate in refrigerator 4 to 5 hours.

For each serving, place 6 to 8 marinated shrimp on greens.

Tossed Greens with Lemon Vinaigrette and Brandied Blossom Fritters

Serves 4 as a main dish or 8 as a side

Greens, shoots, microgreens and herbs all abound in the garden. Whether using a freshly grown or store-bought mix of greens, this is a go-to side or main dish bed. Additions like microgreens, arugula or basil will wake up a plain ol' bag of lettuce any day! Flowers such as pansies, rose petals and nasturtiums make wonderful floral garnishes, too.

Following a Southern tradition of frying just about anything for entertaining, the Brandied Blossom Fritter recipe is a leftover from generations gone by. My Mema (great-grandmother) made these from a cookbook she used, except she would not use beer—she could not be seen, let alone caught, buying beer at the store!

LEMON VINAIGRETTE

Makes about 1 cup

Juice of 2 lemons

½ teaspoon salt

½ teaspoon freshly ground black pepper

2 tablespoons Dijon mustard

1 tablespoon minced garlic

1 tablespoon finely chopped rosemary

3 tablespoons apple cider vinegar

½ cup extra virgin olive oil

Whisk all the vinaigrette ingredients together; taste, and adjust seasonings.

Drizzle the dressing over greens. Garnish with Brandied Blossom Fritters.

Farmer's Note: If using a wooden salad bowl, rub down the inside of the bowl with a peeled garlic clove. Just this light exposure will infuse the salad with that superb flavor!

continued>

BRANDIED BLOSSOM FRITTERS

3 cups fresh blossoms (pansy, viola or rose petals)

2 ounces fruit brandy

2 tablespoons sugar

½ teaspoon cinnamon

1 cup all-purpose flour

1 teaspoon salt

2 egg yolks

2 tablespoons cooking oil

½ cup beer

Water

3 egg whites

Oil for frying

Wash blossoms under cold running water then drain. Spread blossoms on a large platter and sprinkle with brandy, sugar and cinnamon.

Sift flour and salt into a large bowl. In a separate bowl, beat egg yolks lightly and add oil. Stir egg mixture into flour. Add beer gradually and stir until batter is smooth. Add a few drops of lukewarm water to keep batter thin.

In another bowl, beat egg whites until they form peaks, then fold them into the batter.

Heat a good inch of oil in a skillet over medium heat. Dip the blossoms into the batter one at a time, then sauté. Drain and arrange on a serving platter.

Farmer's Note: I found this recipe among some of my great-grandmother's recipes and had to include it. The idea of these petal fritters is much prettier than the actual result. A garnish of petals would be an apropos alternative.

Summer Berries with Mint Whipped Cream

Serves 4

I am fascinated by the accouterments that accompany food. Berries in particular have their own spoons and bowls and even boats (as does gravy). Yet, in all the elegance that can be construed from silver service and fine china, there is hardly anything more elegant than the berries and whipped cream themselves, period. I like to add a splash of mint extract to the cream for an ever-so-delightful flavor boost. And then I like to garnish with mint.

2   pints fresh berries

2   cups heavy whipping cream

½   cup sour cream

Splash of vanilla

2   tablespoons powdered sugar

Pinch of cream of tartar*

½   teaspoon mint extract or more

Mint leaves for garnish, optional

Wash and dry the berries; slice the larger ones if you wish. Divide among four individual dishes.

Whip the two creams together with the vanilla, sugar, cream of tartar and mint extract. Dollop whipped cream on the berries and garnish with mint.

The cream of tartar thickens and also stiffens the creams, and I recommend it only when needing the cream to remain fairly stiff. I actually like the cream to fall and drizzle into the berries.

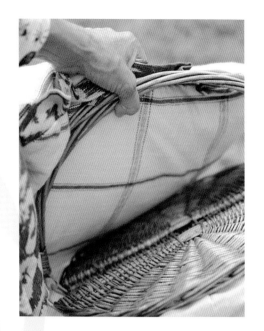

Summer

PICNIC

JTF

Summer Picnic

Ants on a Log

Devilish Deviled Eggs

Goat Cheese Zucchini Roll-Ups

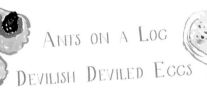

Caprese Panzanella

Pressed Picnic Sandwich

Pasta Salad à la Pepper

Cucumber & Radish Salad

Picnic Parfaits with Granola Crumble & Berries

Mini Brown Sugar Blueberry Pies

The very idea of a picnic fills my mind with memories. Down the street from the home of my great-grandmother, Mema, was a park, where my sisters, cousins and I would play and then picnic under the shade of live oaks. (Note that *picnic* is a noun and a verb.)

Mimi, our grandmother, would make us ants on a log in varied forms for our individual palates: celery stalks with cream cheese and chopped green olives for my sister Maggie; for my baby sister, Meredith, and me, she kept with the peanut butter routine. However, Meredith preferred the sweet and salty combination of peanut butter with apple and raisins; thus Mimi would cater to our every whim—literally cater! Mimi was the best short order cook her grandchildren could have asked for! She could have every dish ready simultaneously for the meal at hand—including a picnic.

It amazes me to think how fortunate my generation is to have had not only our parents but also our grandparents and great-grandparents as part of our childhood. The memory of four generations congregated together for a simple picnic fills my heart with pride and thanksgiving for having been raised so fortunately.

Today's perfect picnic involves not only ants on a log, but a grand sandwich layered with Italian flavors. I've always liked vinegary salads and pickles, so a present-day favorite picnic dish of mine is Cucumber and Radish Salad—sliced ever so thinly. Goat Cheese Zucchini Roll-ups, Pasta Salad à la Pepper, Devilish Deviled Eggs, Heirloom Tomato Panzanella, Picnic Parfaits and Blueberry Picnic Pie round out the menu. Throw in a sundry mix of sodas from not only the South but across the country and a festive array of flavors further makes this picnic charming and refreshing.

I adore jars and have amassed quite a collection. For Southerners, a Mason jar is a multipurpose tool—it is a jar proper, but also a vase, stemware, storage container, serving piece and a picnic must! Other types of jars are perfect for serving individual parfaits or salads, and the very nature of these sorts of jars is what makes them so appealing. The fact that a prepared dish may be serve in, carried in, presented in and consumed from a jar—and look delightful to boot—is proof of the dexterity of a simple jar. I love my picnic basket loaded with them for a very literal dinner on the grounds.

Ants on a Log

Serves 8–10

5 stalks celery

½ cup peanut butter

½ cup cream cheese

¼ cup raisins

¼ cup roughly chopped green olives

Cut celery stalks in half lengthwise and into 4- to 5-inch "logs." Spread half with peanut butter and half with cream cheese. Dot the peanut butter with raisins, and sprinkle the cream cheese with green olives. Press down to stick.

1 large Granny Smith apple

½ cup Nutella

¼ cup salted peanuts

Slice apples, spread on Nutella and top with peanuts. Hardly a better snack has ever been known!

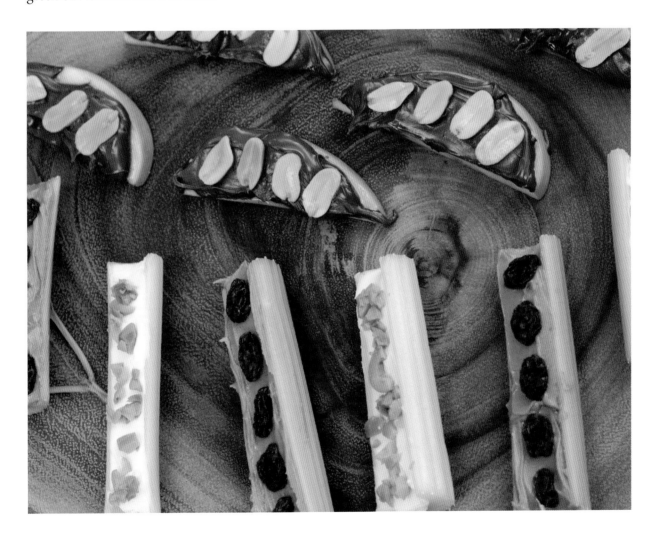

Devilish Deviled Eggs

Serves 10–12

The kick from the relish and the heavy coating of paprika gives these eggs their slightly devilish heat, but it's pretty slight. If you like more of a red devil kick, try adding some red chili pepper.

1 dozen eggs	Kosher salt
2½–3 tablespoons Wickles Relish*	Freshly ground black pepper
4 tablespoons Hellman's mayonnaise	Smoked paprika
1 teaspoon yellow mustard	

Boil eggs. Drain the water and allow eggs to cool in the refrigerator overnight. (That's is the secret to good deviled eggs!)

Shell eggs and slice in half lengthwise; remove yolks to a medium bowl.

Combine egg yolks, relish, mayo, mustard, and salt and pepper to taste. Mix well. (A fork works just fine, but a hand mixer makes a very fluffy mixture.)

Add a tablespoon of filling to each egg half. Garnish generously with paprika.

Or your favorite spicy relish.

Goat Cheese Zucchini Roll-Ups

Serves 8–10

6 medium-to-large zucchini (about 2 pounds), sliced lengthwise ¼ inch thick

Olive oil cooking spray

6 Medjool dates, chopped

8 ounces goat cheese, softened

½ cup shelled unsalted pistachios, toasted and roughly chopped

1 tablespoon fresh lemon juice

2 teaspoons lemon zest

1 tablespoon finely chopped fresh mint

Freshly ground black pepper

Preheat a grill to medium.

Working in batches, lightly mist both sides of zucchini slices with cooking spray and grill for about 3 minutes per side, until softened and lightly charred. Remove and let cool.

In a medium bowl, stir together dates, goat cheese, pistachios, lemon juice, zest and mint. Season to taste with pepper.

Place one slice of zucchini on a clean work surface. Spread 1 teaspoon of the goat cheese mixture onto zucchini and then roll up securely. Transfer to a serving platter, standing up or seam side down (it will stay closed on its own, but a toothpick helps with serving). Repeat with remaining zucchini and goat cheese mixture.

Serve chilled or at room temperature. Do not chill for more than a couple of hours, as the roll-ups will become mushy.

Farmer's Note: On occasion, I have unrolled leftover roll-ups and baked them—makes for a delicious summertime meal or side!

Caprese Panzanella

Serves 6–8

4–5   tablespoons olive oil, divided

3   cups day-old bread cubes
     from baguette

1   teaspoon kosher salt

2   large ripe tomatoes

1   cup yellow cherry tomatoes

2–3   cups diced heirloom tomatoes
     such as 'Brown Berry,' 'Yellow
     Pear' or 'Brandywine'

1   cup loosely packed basil leaves

½   pound fresh mozzarella

Kosher salt

Freshly ground black pepper

In a large sauté pan over medium heat, warm 2–3 tablespoons of the olive oil. Add the bread cubes and salt, and toss. Stir frequently for about 10 minutes, until the cubes are well toasted. Whenever the pan dries out, add a little more olive oil, about a tablespoon at a time. (This is my favorite part of this salad, for the toasted cubes soak up all the goodness from the dressing and tomatoes!) Remove bread cubes from heat and allow them to cool completely.

Cut the cherry tomatoes in half and cut the larger tomatoes into chunks about the same size as the small tomatoes. Combine the two in a large bowl.

Give the basil a couple of rough chops and toss it into the bowl of 'maters.

Cut the mozzarella into cubes and add to the tomato mixture.

Last but not least, add the cooled bread cubes to the bowl (resisting the urge to eat them all immediately). Season to taste with salt and pepper.

VINAIGRETTE DRESSING

¼ cup olive oil

1½ tablespoons white balsamic vinegar

¼ teaspoon Dijon mustard

½ teaspoon finely minced garlic

¼ teaspoon kosher salt

Freshly ground black pepper

Prepare the vinaigrette in a small bowl by whisking together all the ingredients.

Pour the vinaigrette over the salad mixture and toss gently until well incorporated. Allow the salad to sit for just a few minutes so the bread can soak in a little bit of the vinaigrette.

Add a little more salt and freshly ground pepper to taste, and serve immediately.

Farmer's Note: If there are any bread crumbs remaining at the end of your picnic, these will now be totally saturated with the vinegary dressing and absolutely delicious!

Pressed Picnic Sandwich

Serves 4

Olive oil for drizzling, plus 3 tablespoons

1 tablespoon balsamic vinegar

2 cloves garlic, finely chopped

1 teaspoon Dijon mustard

1 12-inch ciabatta loaf, sliced
   in half lengthwise

Sea salt

Generous handful of baby spinach

10 marinated artichoke hearts

Small handful of sundried tomatoes

8 slices prosciutto

Good handful of basil, finely chopped

4–6 slices Pepper Jack cheese

½ medium red onion, very finely sliced

Freshly ground black pepper

In a bowl, whisk together the 3 tablespoons olive oil, balsamic vinegar, garlic and mustard. (The mustard is the emulsifier for the oil and vinegar.) Set aside.

Preheat the oven to 400 degrees.

Place the ciabatta loaf crust side down on a large baking tray and drizzle with a little olive oil and sprinkle with sea salt. Pop the loaf halves into the oven for a few minutes, just until slightly golden and toasted.

Remove the toasted ciabatta halves from the oven and drizzle the base slice with a little bit of the dressing.

Arrange the rest of the ingredients in layers on the ciabatta bread: baby spinach, artichoke hearts, sundried tomatoes, prosciutto, basil, cheese and onion.

Drizzle the rest of the dressing over the sandwich filling and season with salt and pepper to taste. Cap off the sandwich with the top slice of ciabatta and press down.

Wrap in parchment paper and store in the fridge, pressed down with another baking tray filled with heavy items such as cans. You may store the sandwich until ready to serve or overnight. Cut into hearty 3-inch pieces and serve.

Pasta Salad à la Pepper

Serves 6–8

I suggest slightly undercooking your pasta so that it soaks up all the juices and flavors in this dish and doesn't become too mushy. And if you'd like some extra heat, leave the seeds and ribs in the jalapeño.

4 ounces dried whole wheat rotini pasta	1 cup finely chopped red onion
¼ cup freshly squeezed lime juice	1 medium avocado, seeded, peeled, and cut into ½-inch pieces
2 tablespoons olive oil	¾ cup chopped yellow sweet pepper
1 tablespoon sugar	¾ cup chopped red sweet pepper
½ teaspoon salt	1 fresh jalapeño pepper, seeded and finely chopped
½ teaspoon garlic powder	6 bell peppers for serving (red, yellow, orange or a mix), tops removed and hollowed out
½ teaspoon ground cumin	
¼ teaspoon cayenne pepper	
1½ cups grape tomatoes, halved	

Cook pasta according to package directions but just to al dente; drain.

For the dressing, combine the lime juice, oil, sugar, salt, garlic powder, cumin and cayenne pepper in a blender. Cover and blend for about 30 seconds, or until well mixed. Set aside.

In a large bowl, combine pasta, tomatoes, red onion, avocado, sweet peppers and jalapeño pepper. Pour dressing over pasta mixture; toss gently to coat.

Serve in hollowed-out bell peppers.

Cucumber and Radish Salad

Serves 4

My mama loves any salad with cucumbers and a vinegary kick. The interesting earthy heat that radishes present makes this salad a real palate pleaser!

½ cup rice wine vinegar

3 tablespoons sugar

2 tablespoons light oil, such as canola or safflower

1 pound radishes, peeled and thinly sliced

1 English or seedless cucumber, peeled, halved lengthwise and sliced into crescents

4–5 fresh basil leaves, thinly sliced

In a medium bowl, combine vinegar, sugar and oil. Don't hesitate to slightly warm the vinegar to ensure the sugar dissolves completely; a vigorous whisking helps too. Add radishes and cucumber. Toss and combine with basil. Cover and chill until ready to serve.

Farmer's Note: This dish travels well in lidded jars, which also make for lovely serving dishes.

Picnic Parfaits with Granola Crumble and Berries

Makes 4–6 small servings

I love raspberries and use them often. Blackberries, or even the wild plums on our land, are a fun addition. Whatever is in season will taste the best! Apples, pears and pecans make delightful autumnal parfaits too.

1 large container Greek yogurt, vanilla or plain	Fresh berries
Honey	Basic Granola (see below)

Line a mesh strainer with a paper towel and place over a bowl. Stir yogurt, then pour into strainer and place in the fridge for 2 hours. This step ensures a firm parfait that isn't runny.

Pour yogurt into a bowl and stir in honey to taste.

Layer yogurt mixture into small serving vessels with granola, or simply top yogurt with granola and berries.

BASIC GRANOLA

Makes about 4½ cups

I often make this granola for breakfast and snacks. Dried fruits, such as dates, apricots, pineapple, blueberries and apples, make wonderful additions to this granola. They soak up the honey and reconstitute delightfully!

2 cups old-fashioned oats	¼ cup light brown sugar, loosely packed
1 cup sliced almonds or chopped pecans	1½ teaspoons vanilla extract
1 cup shredded coconut, loosely packed*	¾ cup honey
½ cup toasted wheat germ**	¼ teaspoon salt***
3 tablespoons unsalted butter, melted	

Heat oven to 350 degrees. Grease a large baking sheet.

Mix the oats, nuts, coconut and wheat germ with melted butter, sugar and vanilla. Spread over the baking sheet and toast for 10 to 12 minutes, or until the pecans are browned but not burnt. Remove from oven. Glaze with honey and sprinkle with salt.

*Some people don't care for coconut, so if serving to guests, you may want to omit it. I prefer frozen coconut over bagged. It tastes better and stores longer.

**A strange ingredient for Southerners but fabulous to have on hand for recipes such as this. A friend above "the Line" gave me this ingredient tip for granola. I have also used steel-cut oats in lieu of wheat germ. I like the textures of the two different oats.

*** The salt may be incorporated beforehand, but I like the sweet/salty topping of the honey and salt. Flaky sea salt works well too.

Mini Brown Sugar Blueberry Pies

Makes 6

CREAM CHEESE PIE CRUST

- 2 teaspoons cold water
- 1 teaspoon cold cider vinegar
- 1½ cups all-purpose flour, plus more for surface
- ½ teaspoon salt
- 4 ounces (1 stick) cold unsalted butter, cut into small pieces
- 4 ounces cold cream cheese, cut into small pieces
- 6 mini pie cups

Combine water and vinegar in a small bowl. Combine flour and salt in another bowl. Using a pastry cutter or your fingers, cut butter and cream cheese into flour until mixture resembles coarse crumbs with some larger pieces remaining.

Add water mixture to flour mixture in a slow, steady stream, stirring until dough just begins to hold together. (Alternatively, if using a food processor, pulse ingredients.) Turn out the dough onto a piece of lightly floured plastic wrap or wax paper. Section dough into 6 portions and then wrap in plastic. Refrigerate until firm.

Roll out dough pieces and fit into 6 mini pie cups. Trim edges, leaving a slight overhang. Turn overhang under so the edge is flush with the rim of the pie cups. Flute or fork the edges. Freeze until firm, about 15 minutes.

Preheat oven to 350 degrees. Remove pies from the freezer and bake for 20–30 minutes, until golden brown.

BLUEBERRY COMPOTE

- 2 cups fresh blueberries
- ⅓ cup granulated sugar
- ⅓ cup packed brown sugar
- Juice of 1 lemon, preferably Meyer
- ½ fresh vanilla pod
- Mint sprigs, for garnish

In a saucepan over low heat, place about a third of the blueberries, both sugars and lemon juice. Reserve the remaining blueberries.

Using the back of a knife, scrape the vanilla seeds out of the pod and add both seeds and pod to the saucepan. Stir and continue to cook until the blueberries break down and the compote has a syrupy consistency, about 5 to 10 minutes.

Create an ice bath by setting a mixing bowl inside a larger bowl filled with ice. Pour the compote into a strainer over the mixing bowl. Use a rubber spatula to help work the compote through the strainer. Let the compote stand until it is cold to the touch.

Once the blueberry compote has cooled, add the compote to the remaining blueberries and gently mix together to create your pie filling.

Spoon the cooled compote into the pie crusts and voila! Sprigs of mint make beautiful garnishes.

Barn Dinner

IN THE

Mountains

JJF

Barn Dinner
in the Mountains

Basil Blackberry Salad

Baked Tomato "Twists" with Honey & Goat Cheese

Cashiers Farmers Market Pasta

Garlicky Wilted Kale

Toasted Pound Cake

with Peaches, Plums &

Strawberry Sauce

For generations, Southerners have escaped the heat of summertime in the Deep South by retreating to the mountains. For my family and friends, we've found relief in the mountains of western North Carolina. The tiny town of Highlands and its neighboring hamlet, Cashiers, have been sources of great joy, rest, memories and delight since my childhood.

The mountains rejuvenate us wilted Southerners with cool temperatures throughout the summertime, glorious displays of fall foliage, the chance to see snow in wintertime and an extended springtime with dogwood blossoms on tree and shrub forms well into June. These are treats for Deep South dwellers, where our two seasons are "hot" and "not so hot," with a slight respite in between for spring and fall.

Now, I love my homeland and its agrarian and bucolic heritage, but I relish the opportunity to entertain on the grounds of a friend's mountain horse farm or a porch with a view that has no rival. In Cashiers, some good friends have an incredible farmers market purveying the freshest seasonal goodness from the area. Gorgeous vine-ripened tomatoes and even heirloom varieties are piled high. Peaches and plums from the upstate portions of Georgia and South Carolina fill basket after basket at this market. Corn, okra, squash, zucchini, onions, kale, peppers and baked goods all meld into an intoxicating perfume. The barbeque smoke from the side of the market sends the aroma into divinity.

Some friends living in these mountains have a home perched atop a rolling ridge that is surrounded by countryside akin to the pastoral scenes of Kentucky, Virginia and even England. Their barn and grounds were the perfect setting for my Barn Dinner in the Mountains. A menu reflecting the provenance of this area and a gathering of dear friends made this evening ever so lovely.

Through my seasons in the mountains, I am awed and inspired by the produce. Several of the dishes have evolved from forays to the Cashiers Farmers Market, and one dish in particular has become a summertime staple—my Cashiers Farmers Market Pasta. Chock-full of produce and whirled in a wine and butter sauce, this pasta is as delicious the second night as the first, if not more so. A reheat in the oven makes the pasta a tad crispy and slightly roasts the veggies, giving a sensory delight of complementary textures and flavors.

A salad of microgreens, basil and berries from neighboring farms plus some Garlicky Wilted Kale further enhance this farmers market–based menu. A sweet treat of pound cake with peaches and plums and drizzled with strawberry sauce ends the meal on a sweet note—if this mountain community were a song, it would truly be composed of the sweetest notes!

Basil Blackberry Salad

Serves 4–6

1	small log (about 4 ounces) goat cheese
1	heaping teaspoon honey
1–1½	cups microgreens
12	basil leaves, julienned
¾	cup blackberries
1	lemon, halved
1	tablespoon olive oil

In a small bowl, drizzle the goat cheese with honey and mix the two together.

In a medium-size mixing bowl, toss together the microgreens and basil leaves. Add in the blackberries and cheese. Squeeze the juice of both lemon halves over the salad mixture, and then add olive oil. Toss lightly, top with dabs of goat cheese and serve.

Farmer's Note: This is one of my standby summer salads. Since the cheese provides protein, I can eat this salad alone as a meal or with a simple piece of fish or chicken.

Baked Tomato "Twists" with Honey Goat Cheese

Makes a dozen or so

My take on tomato twists, with a honey goat cheese topping, is served in rounds rather than twists. These cheese straw-esque appetizers remind me of a toasted pimento cheese sandwich with vine-ripe tomato. Slicing the dough into rounds makes the prep that much easier, in my opinion, but if you find yourself feeling fancy, well, twist on, my friends!

This recipe came to my family through friends with roots in the tiny town of Concord, North Carolina, which is the familial seat of the Gardin sisters—the Farmer children's best sibling duo of childhood (and now adulthood) friends. Our mothers shared maternity clothes and I cannot remember a time when these siblings were not in my life. I have laughed, played, cried and traveled with these gals my entire life. Plus we've spent some memorable times swapping recipes and eating! I could not ask for dearer friends!

2	cups all-purpose flour, plus extra for the kneading board
2½	teaspoons baking powder
1	teaspoon salt
⅓	cup shortening
¾	cup freshly grated cheese
2	tablespoons celery seed*
⅔	cup tomato juice
¼	cup melted butter

FOR THE HONEY GOAT CHEESE:

1	small (4-ounce) log goat cheese, room temperature
¼–⅓	cup honey
	Sea Salt and freshly ground black pepper, optional
	Dried herbs (such as basil or tarragon), optional

Sift flour, baking powder and salt into a medium-size bowl. Cut in the shortening and cheese until the mixture resembles cornmeal (I use my fingers or a dough cutter, but a food processor works wonderfully too). Add the celery seed and the tomato juice to make a soft dough. Knead the dough on a floured board for 30 seconds. Pat out the dough to ½-inch thickness and cut out rounds. (See Farmer's Note, below.)

Place rounds onto a greased baking sheet. Brush with melted butter and top with celery seeds if not incorporated into the dough. Bake at 450 for 12 to 15 minutes. Serve with honey goat cheese.

To make the honey goat cheese, mix the cheese and honey together and, if desired, season to taste with salt and pepper or dried herbs.

You may incorporate the celery seed into the dough if desired or sprinkle the seeds on top. Baker's choice!

Farmer's Note: Add some finely chopped pecans for crunch—sort of a cheese straw meets pecan sandy!

Cashiers Farmers Market Pasta

Serves 6–8

The first thing I do when I get to Cashiers is stop by the farmers market and gather goodies for this dish. My friends the Crawfords are purveyors of the area's best produce—and barbeque, too. I can buy everything I need at their market for this dish and love that one-stop shopping.

I prepare this dish for a crowd or to feast on by myself for days! It gets better and better with each day, especially if you toast it in the oven to reheat—I really like the crunch factor of toasted pasta and cheese.

1 pound fusilli pasta	2 small zucchini, sliced
½ cup olive oil, plus 1 tablespoon for pasta	2 cups grape tomatoes, halved
8 tablespoons (1 stick) butter	1 heirloom tomato, chopped
½ cup chopped red onion or shallots	1 yellow tomato, chopped
6 medium cloves garlic, minced	2 banana peppers, sliced
2 cups white wine	2 ears white corn, shaved from the cob
2 medium yellow squash, sliced	2 cups grated Pepper Jack cheese
	½ cup chopped green onion

Cook pasta according to package directions. Drain and toss with about 1 tablespoon olive oil to prevent sticking.

In a large skillet, heat olive oil and butter. Brown the onion or shallots. Add in garlic and wine and reduce by one-fourth. Add in squash, zucchini, tomatoes, and banana peppers. Toss and cook until vegetables are tender.

Preheat oven to 400 degrees.

Transfer cooked pasta to a large baking dish. Add the vegetable sauce and corn and toss with the pasta. Top with grated cheese and bake until cheese and pasta are slightly brown and melted. Garnish with green onion.

Season with salt and pepper.

Garlicky Wilted Kale

Serves 4

My baby sister, Meredith, loves kale. Whether wilted, baked into chips or tossed into a soup or pasta, she loves this green. Her "brubbs" does too!

2 small bundles kale leaves	2 tablespoons minced garlic
½ cup olive oil	Sea salt and freshly ground black pepper
10–12 whole cloves garlic	Lemon juice, optional

Remove the thick stems and ribs from the kale leaves and chop leaves into thirds.

In a large skillet over low heat, warm olive oil. Toss in garlic cloves and carefully brown both sides. Remove the garlic and set aside.

Add the kale and minced garlic to the oil. Wilt kale in the oil over medium-to-low heat. Add salt and pepper to taste.

Remove kale from the skillet with tongs.* Spread wilted kale on a serving dish and garnish with browned garlic cloves. Add a squeeze of lemon juice, if desired.

Reserve the garlic-infused oil for salad dressing, a dip for bread, or for sautéing veggies and meat. It stores indefinitely in an airtight jar.

Toasted Pound Cake with Plums, Peaches and Strawberry Sauce

Serves 6–8

I love the strawberry sauce from Cashiers Farmers Market, but when I'm home in the country, I make my own using fresh or frozen berries.

8 tablespoons (1 stick) butter, room temperature

½ cup Crisco solid shortening

2½ cups sugar

6 large eggs, room temperature

3 cups all-purpose flour, sifted

½ pint (1 cup) whipping cream

1 teaspoon vanilla extract

Strawberry Sauce (see below)

Plum wedges

Peach wedges

Butter and flour a tube or Bundt pan.

Cream the butter and Crisco with the sugar until fluffy. Add the eggs one at a time, beating well after each addition.

Add the flour to the batter alternately with the cream, beginning and ending with flour. Stir in the vanilla.

Pour the batter into prepared baking pan and place into a cold oven. Turn heat to 300 degrees and cook for 75 minutes. Reduce heat to 325 degrees and cook another 15 minutes to brown the top, or until a skewer inserted into the cake comes out clean. Allow the cake to cool for a few minutes.

Turn out the cake upside down onto a plate, if you wish, then use another plate to turn it back over. Which should be the actual top of the pound cake is debatable and will depend on how your cake looks. I like the top that was the top in the oven. When ready to serve, toast slices of pound cake in the oven. Top with Strawberry Sauce and serve with fruit wedges.

STRAWBERRY SAUCE

Makes about 2 cups

2 cups chopped strawberries

¾–1 cup sugar, to taste

2 tablespoons fresh lemon juice

½ teaspoon vanilla extract

Place all the ingredients in a medium-size bowl and fold until the sugar is fully incorporated; then let sit for about 10 minutes, stirring every few minutes, until the strawberries release their juice and a sauce forms.

Dinner
ON THE Dock

JTF

Dinner on the Dock

Oysters Bluffton

Summer Squash with Feta & Thyme

Peach Salad with Honey Goat Cheese

& White Balsamic Dressing

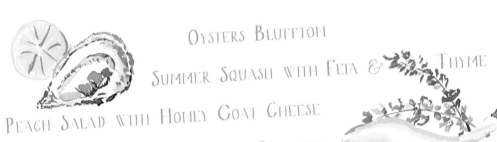

Squash & Corn Pudding

Country Sausage Dogs

with Mimi's Mustard Sauce & Relish

Peach Tart with Rosemary Crust

Though the farmlands of Middle Georgia are my home, the Carolina Lowcountry sirens a welcoming song to my heart every time I visit. The history, heritage, customs and genteel, natural beauty of this locale have made their marks on my psyche, and so I feel quite at home and at peace there.

The May River lulls into the marshes of the Carolina Lowcountry, blending seamlessly into a lacy, feathered edge of earth and water. Here, spartina grass, palmetto, live oak, myrtle and magnolia canopy the landscape, creating a dense habitat for fish and fowl. A myriad of wildlife on the turf and in the surf abides within this sanctuary, thus providing an abundance of choices for menus.

Some dear friends of mine have a dock that jetties into the deeper waters of the May River, where dolphins feed, owls and herons fly by, fish swarm and crabs crawl. Oyster rakes are exposed with the waning of the tide. My menu for dinner on the dock celebrates friendship and reflects the Lowcountry's bounty as well as its people's cultural heritage.

Oysters Bluffton start the dinner—in true Blufftonian fashion. The May River is known for its tasty oysters, thus Blufftonian fashion for consumption is to eat them "naked," or without any dressing. Shucked and served perhaps with lemon, saltines and hot sauce is the only way, for this river town!

A salad of mixed greens and herbs with peaches, goat cheese and honey cleanses the palate. Yellow crookneck squash in two fashions make up the sides. I know, two squash dishes may make this menu seem repetitive, but they are so different from one another that your family and friends won't mind a bit. If your garden is anything like mine, you'll be thrilled for recipes aplenty for squash aplenty!

A main course of Country Sausage Dogs reflects the agrarian and hunting customs of the region. For dessert, a Rosemary-Peach Tart lusciously topped with Sour Cream Whipped Cream.

I hope you find a place of tranquility and serene natural beauty such as I have found in the Carolina Lowcountry. Truly, it is places like this tangled stretch of land and sea—with the famed, enchanting cities of Charleston and Savannah standing like sentries at each end—where both body and soul are fed and nourished.

Summer Squash with Feta and Thyme

Serves 4

Feta and thyme are a melodious duo. I find myself using them as accompaniments to salads and savory dishes alike, but this may be my favorite use. The feta browns deliciously, and the bit of crunch from the breadcrumbs combined with the soft squash is a textural delight.

In the fall I like to use acorn, butternut or even spaghetti squash in this meal. My thyme is usually still in good shape come autumn, but I've found that sage works wonderfully in this dish as well.

½ tablespoon butter

1 tablespoon olive oil

1 small Vidalia or red onion, chopped

4–6 small-to-medium summer squash, sliced into rounds

Pinch of salt

Pinch of pepper

⅓ cup crumbled feta cheese

1 generous teaspoon dried thyme or 1 tablespoon fresh thyme

3 tablespoons (or more) panko breadcrumbs or Ritz crackers crumbs

Heat butter and olive oil in a cast-iron skillet or ovenproof pan. Add onion and cook until browned. Add squash slices and salt and pepper to taste, then sauté until tender. Sprinkle with feta crumbles, thyme, and breadcrumbs, then transfer skillet to a preheated 375-degree oven. Cook until topping is slightly browned and feta is warmed, about 5 minutes.

Peach Salad with Honey Goat Cheese and White Balsamic Dressing

Serves 2–4

Peaches and balsamic are a riveting duet of flavors. Combining them with other flavors in this salad, or in any dish, is such a complement to all the ingredients. The creamy goat cheese and earthy greens all blend together well too. I adore this salad all summer long. Apples and pears make great fall additions in lieu of peaches. Grapefruit and oranges are perfect in the winter, as are spring berries for that season.

1 tablespoon honey	Small handful basil leaves, torn (about ½–¾ cup)
1 small log (4 ounces) goat cheese	Small handful mint leaves (about ½ cup)
16 ounces mixed greens (any combination of baby spinach and spring butter or Bibb lettuces)	2 peaches,* sliced into wedges
	White Balsamic Dressing (see below)

In a small bowl, pour the honey over the goat cheese and allow cheese to soften. Mix the two together and set aside.

In a salad bowl, toss in mixed greens, basil, mint, and peaches. Top with dollops of honey goat cheese. Pour dressing over the salad and lightly toss.

Pears are a delicious substitute for peaches in the fall and winter.

WHITE BALSAMIC DRESSING

3 tablespoons white balsamic vinegar	Pinch of salt
½ cup olive or pecan oil	Pinch of pepper
Pinch of sugar	

Whisk together dressing ingredients and set aside until ready to use.

Farmer's Note: This dressing is intentionally mild to allow the salad flavors to stand out. If desired, you may amp up the vinegar for more flavor.

Squash and Corn Pudding

Serves 2–4

I am slightly embarrassed by how much I adore this dish. If allowed, I could eat the entire pan of this pudding without thinking twice about it! The mild pepper flavor, the silkiness of the squash and the sweetness of the corn meld into a dish that I crave throughout the warm months.

In the South, green bell peppers keep coming in from the garden well into fall. I have found that combining them with autumn squashes like acorn and butternut make a delightful Squash and Corn Pudding. This dish travels well, freezes well and presents ever so well. The fresher and more flavorful the produce, the better the flavor. Leftovers reheated to a golden brown the next day make a superb lunch.

4	tablespoons butter, divided		Oil, optional
1	green bell pepper, slivered	1	egg
¼	cup all-purpose flour	½	cup milk
2	cups summer squash, sliced	1	tablespoon sugar
1	cup water or chicken broth	½	teaspoon salt
2	cups corn freshly cut from cobs		Freshly ground black pepper
1	large onion, sliced		

Melt 2 tablespoons butter in a saucepan. Sauté slivered green pepper until just soft. Add flour and stir until well blended with the butter. Set aside.

Cook squash in a small amount of water or chicken broth until tender, about 6 to 8 minutes. Drain and mash. Set aside.

Cook corn and onion together in remaining butter, or substitute oil, until tender. For a more pudding-like texture, blanch for 2 minutes, then drain and slightly mash the corn and onion. I like a bit of crunch, or slightly tender corn.

In a bowl, beat egg and milk together. Combine with pepper-flour mixture and add the sugar and salt. Fold the corn into the mashed squash, then turn into a baking dish and bake in a preheated 350-degree oven for 30 minutes, or until slightly brown on top.

Garnish the pudding with freshly cracked black pepper to taste at the table. This insures that the pepper flavor is fresh rather than baked in.

Country Sausage Dogs with Mimi's Mustard Sauce and Relish

Serve at least one bun-length link per person

The Lowcountry, as with much of the South, relies on a steady supply of pork for many dishes. Chops, tenderloins, hams, bacons and sausages fill our larders and bellies all throughout the year.

One of the foods my family has always served is the sausage dog. Instead of a hot dog, a grilled piece of country sausage from M&T Meats or Stripling's is the mainstay at our barbeques and cookouts. Venison versions of the sausage dog also have a place in our repertoire, since many of the menfolk in my family (and most Southern families) are hunters. Smoked or spicy, mild or stuffed, sausage is an anytime option for meals. With a biscuit in the morning or on a bun for lunch or dinner, sausage seems to satisfy every appetite.

A few suggestions for your dogs: Grill bun-length links of your favorite pork or venison sausage—a bit of charring is tasty and makes for a great complement to a soft bun. (I like to steam the buns to make them even softer.) For added heat, try spicy sausage or top your regular sausage dog with sliced peppers. I take mine with a bit of yellow mustard or piled high with Mimi's Mustard Sauce and some sort of relish. If Mimi was making a batch of bread and butter pickles, those were my relish of choice. However, I love the sweet spiciness of Wickles pickles, so their relish is a favorite too.

MIMI'S MUSTARD SAUCE

Makes about 1½ cups

A ramped-up version of my grandmother's famous sauce kicks up the flavor in any dish. My family especially enjoys it with sausage, but it is just as delicious on burgers, chicken and pork or as a dip for fries. You can even use it for basting fish, pork or chicken in the oven. Enjoy, y'all!

1 cup mayonnaise	1 teaspoon yellow mustard
½ cup ketchup	1 teaspoon Dijon mustard
Juice from ½ small lemon	1 teaspoon grainy mustard
1 teaspoon Morton Nature's Seasons Seasoning Blend	½ teaspoon dry mustard
½ teaspoon minced garlic	Touch of honey
	Freshly ground black pepper

In a small mixing bowl, thoroughly mix all the ingredients together and adjust seasonings to taste. Sauce can be stored for a week in the refrigerator.

Peach Tart with Rosemary Crust

Serves 8

A meal that starts and ends with peaches is not bad at all. However, another perk of this recipe is how adaptable it is to the seasons. Apples and pears make for perfect fall and winter tarts. Pecans, walnuts or even thyme can also be mixed into the dough for a seasonal flair. Dried cranberries are delicious with the apples or pears, and blueberries or plums make scrumptious spring and summertime alternatives. Master this dish and you'll have a dessert for any season.

I can hardly get enough of the combination that peaches and rosemary bring to the table. I like to serve the tart with ice cream or my Sour Cream Whipped Cream. (This tart makes a perfect breakfast treat too!)

FOR THE TART DOUGH:

- 2 cups all-purpose flour
- ½ teaspoon salt
- 1 tablespoon sugar
- 1 tablespoon dried rosemary or 2 tablespoons fresh, roughly chopped
- 12 tablespoons (1½ sticks) cold butter
- ½ cup ice water

Combine the dry ingredients, including the rosemary, with your fingers in a large mixing bowl. If using a food processor, then just pulse to mix.

Slice the butter into cubes and mix into the flour with a hand mixer or pulse in food processor until the dough begins to clump and the butter is pea-size or smaller.

Slowly pour the ice water into the mixture, continuing to mix until a ball of dough is formed. On a floured surface, roll the dough into a large disk. Wrap in plastic wrap and chill in the refrigerator for about an hour.

Roll or spread out the chilled dough into your desired shape. For me, the rustic feel of an imperfect circle or rectangle is what makes the simple elegance of this dessert so pretty.

FOR THE TART FILLING:

- 4–6 fresh peaches, peeled and cut into wedges
- ½ cup sugar (raw, vanilla, or plain)

Arrange the peach slices on the dough in whatever fashion you wish. Cover peaches with the sugar, adjusting the amount to suit the sweetness of the fruit and your own sweet tooth.

FOR THE GLAZE:

Peach jam or preserves

Bake the tart in a preheated 350-degree oven for about 45 minutes, or until the dough is golden brown. While the tart is still warm, use a pastry brush to glaze with peach jam or preserves. Serve with dollops of peach jam or preserves and Sour Cream Whipped Cream—the perfect palate-pleasing accompaniment!

SOUR CREAM WHIPPED CREAM

1½ cups heavy whipping cream

¾ cup sour cream

2 tablespoons sugar (plain, vanilla or powdered)

1 teaspoon vanilla extract

½ teaspoon vanilla beans scraped from a pod, optional*

By hand, with a hand mixer or stand mixer, whip together the two creams, sugar, vanilla extract and vanilla beans, if using, until soft peaks form. Sweeten more or less as desired; I like it not too sweet, and the tang from the sour cream is lovely. Serve over just about anything!

*For added flavor depth and texture.

Birthday Dinner
IN *Highlands*

JFF

Birthday Dinner
in Highlands

Roasted Medley of Potatoes & Onions

Dilly-Creamed Corn Cornbread

Brie and Cucumber Salad with Mahaw Dressing

Sautéed Summer Peas

Bacon-Wrapped Pork Tenderloin

Grown-Up Dirt Cake

ot everyone can have their best bud marry their sister. I, though, am one such claimant. My brother-in-law, Zach, is as fine a gentleman as can be. We share the same hometown, a love for nature and even had the same major in college. We both treasure and respect our families and traditions and, most importantly, we both love Maggie. I don't think I could have married off my sister to anyone else!

Zach and I also share a fondness for the mountains. His maternal grandparents retired to the Appalachias, and he grew up camping, fishing and hiking their woods, streams and trails. What better grounds to dine upon and celebrate this friend, brother, husband and father than the same grounds that hold such memory and joy for him.

With Zach's love for gardening and nature, his birthday dinner was set on the grounds of a dear friend's home and garden, nestled near the crests, ridges and plateaus of North Carolina's Blue Ridge Mountains—what I like to call my "happy place." Here, an array of evergreens, such as rhododendron, hemlock, mountain laurel and spruce, create a backdrop for the autumnal riot of color provided by the deciduous hardwoods of oak, maple, birch and walnut.

The sky is a rich, clear blue, not muffled with the humidity and hazy heat of our native portion of Georgia. Rudbeckias, daisies, creeping roses, phlox, hydrangeas and lilies bloom all summer long, after the dogwood, Kousa dogwood, rhododendron and mountain laurel bloom in spring and early summer. Hostas, huechera and ferns all add to the constant evergreens and weave a lush greenness into this landscape. Velvety smooth fescue grass gives this woodland garden a unique fullness with its blanket of green.

To celebrate Zach's birthday, I planned a menu hopefully fitting his taste and range of culinary enjoyment—with a bit of whimsy for dessert. Happy birthday to the best buddy and brother I could ask for!

Roasted Medley of Potatoes and Onions

Serves 4

Roasted vegetables are simply the best! You can dress this dish with balsamic vinegar, a dollop of sour cream or sautéed mushrooms. It's hard to beat the fabulous combo of potatoes and onions.

Bacon drippings*

1 large sweet potato, cut into 1-inch cubes

½ dozen baby red potatoes

½ dozen Baby Dutch Yellow potatoes

1 large Vidalia onion, sliced into wedges (red, chipotle or other onions all work well too)

Sea salt and freshly ground black pepper

¼ cup chopped green onion, chives or ramps

Preheat oven to 450 degrees.

Add enough bacon drippings to cover the bottom of a large iron skillet or baking dish. Add the potatoes and onions to the skillet and season to taste with salt and pepper. Roast for 25 to 30 minutes, or until potatoes are golden and wilted and onions are caramelized.

Garnish with green onion, chives or ramps.

Any decent, well-raised Southern cook has a jar of bacon drippings handy.

Dilly Creamed Corn Cornbread

Serves 4–6

THE FARMER'S SKILLET CORN WITH DILL

3 pieces thick-cut bacon	1 cup sweet milk or cream*
1 Vidalia onion, diced	Sea salt
4 cups whole kernel Silver Queen corn (about 6 ears) cut from the cob	Cracked Black Pepper
	3 sprigs dill, roughly chopped

On medium heat, render and brown the bacon in an iron skillet. Once bacon is browned, remove from drippings and allow to cool.

Cook the onion in the bacon drippings until the onion becomes translucent and starts to show some brown around the edges.

Add the corn. Stir continually for 5 minutes, tossing the corn with the onions and drippings. (**Caution:** Iron skillets get very hot, so you may have to reduce the heat during this step to avoid scorching the corn. The drippings help coat it and minimize scorching, but do mind the heat.) Corn should still be crisp and not mushy.

Reduce heat to low and stir the milk or cream into the onion and corn mixture. Season to taste with salt and pepper, then add dill and stir. Allow cream to bubble and thicken a bit. Reserve until the cornbread batter is mixed.

*Whole milk, heavy cream, buttermilk or half-and-half all work just fine.

BIG PAN O' CORNBREAD

2 cups self-rising white cornmeal*

1 cup self-rising flour

2 eggs

1¼ cups buttermilk, plus a bit
   more to thin the batter

2 tablespoons vegetable oil, plus
   1 tablespoon for the pan

Pinch of sugar

Preheat oven to 400 degrees.

Mix above ingredients into a batter. Fold in the Farmer's Skillet Corn with Dill and turn out into a hot, oiled iron skillet. Bake for 20 minutes. Serve hot with butter.

Farmer's Note: Sugar added to cornbread is not typically a part of the Southern culinary repertoire; yet, I've found that a pinch takes the bite out of the buttermilk's punch and levels out the dill, too.

Martha White or White Lily—we are in Dixie, after all.

Brie and Cucumber Salad with Mayhaw Dressing

Serves 4–6

Texture, texture, texture—I am all about the texture when it comes to salads. I love a chopped salad when every item is cut to the same size, but I also relish a salad with the same ingredients prepared differently. Case in point, this salad.

My buddy Chef Jason Whitaker is the head chef at the Chattooga Club in Cashiers. This man can fry the best chicken (next to Mimi and Mrs. Mary) and bake biscuits that I'm sure St. Peter will offer at the Pearly Gates. Chef Jason also prepares a salad with locally grown produce; it changes weekly with the progressing seasons. At Chattooga, I delighted in the singsong of the cucumber and cheese and the crispness of the greens, and I simply had to applaud the tie that bound it all together—a mayhaw dressing. If you need to know what a mayhaw is, y'all come down South for a spell. Best I can tell you— it's a persimmon-type fruit close to a pawpaw.

Back to my admiration for texture: I re-created Chef Jason's salad—this time with some ingredients shaved, sliced and chopped. I rest my apron, iron skillet and any culinary prowess when it comes to out-cooking Chef Jason, but I can sure try to imitate his work. My sincerest flattery, bud!

½ cup shaved red onion*

½–1 cup shaved Granny Smith apple

About 1½ cups mixed microgreens and other greens of choice

1 wheel Green Hill Cheese from Sweet Grass Dairy, cut into 4 wedges

¼ cup shaved cucumber

¼ cup cucumber rounds

MAYHAW DRESSING

Makes about ¾ cup

Juice of ½ lemon

1 tablespoon minced garlic

½ teaspoon microplaned red onion**

1 teaspoon Dijon mustard

¼ teaspoon salt

¼ teaspoon cracked black pepper

¼ teaspoon Morton Nature's Seasons Seasoning Blend

½ cup olive or pecan oil

1 teaspoon finely chopped seasonal herbs***

3 tablespoons mayhaw jelly****

Plate the salad ingredients or toss together in a large bowl.

Whisk all the dressing ingredients together. If the jelly isn't mixing well with the other ingredients, warm the dressing slightly to help the jelly dissolve. Pour dressing over salad and serve.

*A vegetable peeler works fine, as does a mandolin.

**I think that onion "paste," as it becomes when mircoplaned, is the secret to making so many dishes absolutely divine.

***For summertime, I love basil and mint or thyme. For springtime, I prefer parsley and chervil. For fall, rosemary or sage are my favorites.

****As with the herbs, you can change the jelly flavor seasonally.

Sautéed Summer Peas

Serves 6–8

Another fine characteristic of brother-in-law Zach is that he, like yours truly, does not care for mushy vegetables. We both agree that vegetables lose their flavor when overcooked. We also agree that part of the joy of eating a variety of veggies is the wide range of textures brought to the table. This dish is a quick sauté, a go-to side dish for any meal—and it makes a fantastic presentation too.

2	cups sugar snap peas		Splash of vinegar or red wine
2	cups lady peas		Salt and pepper
	Olive oil	¼	cup shaved red onion

In a sauté pan, iron skillet or enameled iron skillet, sauté peas with olive oil, vinegar, and salt and pepper to taste until peas are only slightly crunchy. This just takes a few minutes. Finish off with a healthy splash of vinegar or wine and toss the peas a couple more times. Serve garnished with the red onion.

Bacon-Wrapped Pork Tenderloin

Serves 4–6

Pork wrapped in pork—what a dream! Bacon as a wrapping on just about anything is perfection. This tenderloin combo is a celebration meal in our family. The menfolk, especially, clamor for these dishes; thus, this particular tenderloin has become a party favorite for the boys' birthdays.

2 pork tenderloins (3 pounds total) each cut in half	1 tablespoon wine vinegar or white vinegar
1 pound bacon	¼ teaspoon salt
¾ cup soy sauce	Dash of freshly ground black pepper
1 tablespoon minced onions	¾ cup brown sugar
½ teaspoon garlic salt	1 tablespoon honey
	1 teaspoon crushed red pepper flakes

Wrap tenderloin pieces in bacon. Place in an 8½ x 11-inch pan. Poke holes in the pork loins with a fork.

Combine the remaining ingredients in a small bowl and stir well. Pour marinade over meat. Refrigerate tightly covered for 2 to 3 hours or overnight.

Preheat oven to 300 degrees. Bake tenderloins for 2 to 3 hours. If bacon starts to burn, place foil over the top after approximately 1½ hours of baking. When done, remove from oven, cut meat into small slices and allow meat to soak up the excess juices in the pan.

Grown-Up Dirt Cake

Serves 10–12

What makes a dirt cake "grown up?" Kahlua—that's what! No instant pudding, jelly worms or fake flowers here. This "dirt" is rich! Completely apropos for a gardener like Zach.

The very process of making a homemade chocolate cake and buttermilk chocolate pudding makes this a dish of devotion. You can cheat and use a cake mix and dairy whip, but, trust me, the flavor depth of homemade is much greater. I love how coffee brings out the flavor of the chocolate but doesn't flavor the cake. When you are eating something as decadent as this, go all out and don't cut corners!

1	Farmer's Basic Chocolate Cake, cooled and cut into cubes (see below)	12	ounces Sour Cream Whipped Cream (see page 103)
½–¾	cup Kahlua (it's your party, add another splash if you'd like)	1	Skor candy bar, broken into small pieces*
	Buttermilk Chocolate Puddin' (see page 120)		

Assemble in a trifle dish or glass bowl or layer on individual dessert plates. Drizzle cake layers with Kahlua. (Serve more as an aperitif or drink!)

Arrange in layers of cake squares, pudding and whipped cream, ending with whipped cream and sprinkling with broken bits of Skor bar.

A Butterfinger or a few Reese's cups will also work.

THE FARMER'S BASIC CHOCOLATE CAKE

2	cups sugar	2	eggs, room temperature
1¾	cups all-purpose flour, sifted	1	cup buttermilk, well shaken
¾	cup Hershey's cocoa	½	cup vegetable oil
1½	teaspoons baking powder	2	teaspoons high-quality vanilla extract
1½	teaspoons baking soda	1	cup hot coffee
1	teaspoon salt		

Preheat oven to 350 degrees. Grease and flour two 9-inch round baking pans (or a 9 x 13-inch baking dish if assembling a trifle).

continued>

Combine all the dry ingredients in a large bowl. Add wet ingredients, except coffee, and beat for 2 minutes. Add the cup of hot coffee—the batter will be thin.

Divide the batter between the two pans (if making a layer cake) and bake about 30 minutes, until a toothpick inserted in the center comes out clean.

Allow the cakes to cool for about 10 minutes and then remove them from their pans.

BUTTERMILK CHOCOLATE PUDDIN'

Serves 6 if not being used for the trifle

- ¼ cup cornstarch
- ½ cup sugar
- ⅛ teaspoon salt
- 2½ cups whole milk

- ½ cup buttermilk
- 6 ounces 60% good-quality semisweet chocolate,* coarsely chopped
- 1 teaspoon pure vanilla extract

Combine the cornstarch, sugar and salt in the top of a double boiler. Slowly whisk the milks into the mixture, scraping the bottom and sides with a heatproof spatula to incorporate into the dry ingredients. Place over gently simmering water and cook for 15 to 20 minutes, stirring occasionally and continuing to scrape the bottom and sides (use a whisk as necessary if lumps begin to form). When the mixture begins to thicken and coats the back of a spoon, add the chocolate. Continue stirring for about 2 to 4 minutes, until the pudding is smooth and thickened. Remove from the heat and stir in the vanilla.

Strain through a fine-mesh strainer (if you feel confident there are no lumps, skip this step) into a serving bowl. Cover with plastic wrap pushed onto the top of the pudding to prevent a skin from forming. Refrigerate for at least 30 minutes.

Use 70% bittersweet if you want more of a dark chocolate kick.

Fireside Dinner ON THE Mountain

J F F

Fireside Dinner
on the Mountain

Oven-Poached Salmon

Roasted Okra

Roasted Squash & Zucchini

Skillet Toast

Sweet Potato Wedges with   Rosemary Butter

Honey-Lemon Olive Oil Cake

Amaretto Peach Bake

*S*ummer nights in the mountains can provide a jewel that many Southern nights cannot offer at lower altitudes—an evening fire on the porch. When nighttime temperatures in the mountains drop, a summer evening becomes crisp and fall-like. Having a fireplace on your porch allows you to enjoy each and every second of the fabulous climate these altitudes afford. A simple meal, a lovely setting and some wonderful fellowship with friends or family make a fireside dinner on the mountain that much more enjoyable.

For such evenings, I have a go-to menu that is quick, healthy and easy to prepare; thus, no time is wasted in the kitchen while the fire blazes and the mountains are glowing in the distance. The Cashiers Farmers Market and other purveyors of delicious foodstuffs in the Cashiers and Highlands area have direct connections for wonderful seafood. Fish, shrimp and scallops are caught and carried up the mountains on special runs, giving patrons a variety of seafood from which to choose. It may seem ironic to eat seafood in the mountains, but the opportunity for freshly caught fish has folks in line at these markets! The local rainbow trout, too, is a famed part of the culinary legacy here (and may be substituted in the salmon recipe).

This particular dinner steps up from the grounds and onto the porch. As darkness falls and cooler temperatures claim the air, a dinner on the grounds is achieved by a dinner on the porch. Add the ambiance of a crackling fire and the evening instantly becomes memorable and truly remarkable and enchanting.

Oven-poached in white wine, the salmon cooks quickly but retains its delicate flavor and flaky texture; garden herbs and a touch of lemon add a refreshing element to the dish. Roasting vegetables brings out their natural sugars, thus charring and caramelizing the outside—yielding a flavor that complements most any main dish. Summertime brings about an abundance of vegetables suitable for roasting, okra being a favorite of mine. Sliced lengthwise, crispy skewered okra is simply fabulous with any meal, especially a fireside dinner.

Since this meal is all oven-cooked, why break the course of action? Roasted rounds of squash and zucchini with some jalapeño heat add to the menu's prowess. Some toasted bread from the farmers market and baked peaches or apples top off the meal. Two fires—one on the porch and the other from the oven—make this a wonderful meal.

Oven-Poached Salmon

Serves 4–6

My Montgomery mamas, Laura Harmon and Melissa Wilson, are wonderful cooks and hostesses. They have both taught me so much about entertaining and cooking—specifically, to be confident and have fun with it. Being able to entertain on a moment's notice is an admirable trait possessed by these two women. This dish is a quick solution to the age-old question "What's for dinner?" and can be easily called into service for last-minute company. Whether you are feeding the masses or just yourself, this Oven-Poached Salmon will hit the spot! Come to think of it, this recipe might have come from Mr. Harmon.

1 portioned salmon filet per person

About ¼ cup olive oil

1 teaspoon salt

1 teaspoon pepper

1 lemon, sliced into thin rounds

2–4 sprigs fresh dill per filet

3–4 cups good white wine

Preheat oven to 425 degrees.

Place salmon filets in a rectangular baking dish, skin side down. Drizzle filets with olive oil and season with salt and pepper to taste.

Top the filets with the lemon slices.

Cover generously with dill sprigs.

Pour white wine over filets (wine should fill the pan up about 1 inch) and cover loosely with foil.

For a medium-rare filet, bake for 8 to 10 minutes, or until filets are flaky yet still tender. Add 2 minutes for medium and 4 minutes for a well-done piece of salmon.

Farmer's Note: Filets of rainbow trout or any kind of fresh trout may be substituted for the salmon in this recipe.

Roasted Okra

Serves 4

No Southern garden or summertime supper is complete without okra. I love okra boiled, fried, baked, roasted and mixed with tomatoes and served over rice with tomatoes. This roasting technique, though, may be my favorite!

By roasting the okra with its sliced side up, more surface area is exposed for caramelization. This browning of the natural sugars and starches in okra and other vegetables is what makes roasting my go-to method of cooking. Since science and chemistry are taking care of the flavor with the oven's heat, olive oil, salt and pepper are all you need for roasting. Other ingredients gild the lily, for sure, but the natural flavors brought about by roasting and caramelizing fruits and vegetables are second to none.

About 4 cups fresh okra

2 tablespoons olive oil

1 teaspoon salt

1 teaspoon pepper

Preheat oven to 425 degrees.

Slice okra in half lengthwise and arrange on a cookie sheet cut side up—or alternating cut side up and down makes for a beautiful presentation. Drizzle with olive oil and sprinkle with salt and pepper.

Roast okra until golden brown, about 12 minutes.

Roasted Squash and Zucchini

Serves 4–6

My roasting moxie bodes true for squash and zucchini as well. Adding some rounds of jalapeño (with seeds) will ensure this dish is a fiery one! Beware—those seeds will light up your taste buds; remove them if you are sensitive to heat.

2 yellow squash, cut into rounds	1 teaspoon salt
2 zucchini, cut into rounds	1 teaspoon pepper
2 jalapeño peppers, cut into rounds	½ teaspoon red pepper flakes
1 tablespoon olive oil	

Preheat oven to 425 degrees.

Place squash, zucchini, and jalapeño rounds on a large cookie sheet.

Drizzle with olive oil and sprinkle with salt, pepper, and red pepper flakes.

Roast until golden brown.

Skillet Toast

Mimi had an aunt in Savannah who had toast and hot tea every morning for breakfast. Mimi decided that this would be her morning menu, as well, and rarely strayed from it. Toasting in the oven is one thing, but the flavor rendered from an iron skillet sauté, mind you, is another—especially when a dry piece of bread soaks up the oil from a well-seasoned skillet! I dare you to toast your bread in the oven or a toaster again!

1 loaf of your favorite artisan-style bread, sliced

About 3 tablespoons olive oil

Heat olive oil in a cast-iron or a heavy-bottomed skillet. Brown each slice of bread on both sides. Add more oil if making more than about 4 slices.

Sweet Potato Wedges with Rosemary Butter

Serves 4

Sweet potatoes are cornerstones of the Southern culinary tradition. In fact, the state of Louisiana touts them as "yams" and their advertising cards, posters and signage from the late 19th to early 20th century have become collectors' items. Sweet potatoes, to me, are highly versatile. Amazingly healthy on their own, with vitamins and nutrients abounding, they are easily embellished with sweet and savory ingredients of all sorts.

I adore using them to make a sweet potato biscuit, as the filler for a pie, as the base for a BBQ-piled main dish or a myriad other concoctions. Here, I slice the sweet potatoes into wedges and serve them with a savory rosemary butter. The flavor combo of sweet potato and rosemary is classic and reminds me of fall and wintertime meals as a child.

We had a big batch of rosemary growing strong near the kitchen door of the farmhouse. The smell alone makes me think of walking in and out of that door, and the flavor reminds me of times at the farmhouse too. From apple pie to tea and lemonade to beef, pork and chicken, I find ways to use rosemary.

1½	tablespoons olive oil, divided	½	teaspoon black pepper
2–4	medium-to-large sweet potatoes		Rosemary Butter with Lemon and Garlic (see page 134)
1	teaspoon salt		

Grease a roasting pan or baking sheet with about ½ tablespoon of olive oil. Preheat the oven to 475, or even up to 500 if your oven allows.

Cut each sweet potato lengthwise into about 8 wedges and toss with salt, pepper, and remaining 1 tablespoon oil in a large bowl. Arrange potato wedges flat sides down on baking sheet, then cover pan tightly with foil and roast for 10 minutes at 500 degrees (12 minutes at 475 degrees). Remove foil and roast 10 minutes more. Loosen potatoes with a spatula, then turn over onto other flat side and roast until tender and golden, about another 10 minutes. Total cooking time is about 30 minutes.

Remove potatoes from the oven, loosen with spatula, then transfer to a serving dish or plates. Slice rosemary butter into thin rounds and serve over the sweet potatoes.

continued>

ROSEMARY BUTTER WITH LEMON AND GARLIC

Makes 8 tablespoons

8 tablespoons (1 stick) unsalted butter, room temperature

½–1 teaspoon chopped fresh rosemary

1 teaspoon lemon zest

½ teaspoon chopped garlic

Dash of salt (I like about ½ teaspoon of coarse sea salt for texture)

Dash of freshly cracked black pepper

In a mixing bowl, mix the butter with the rosemary, zest, garlic, salt and pepper.

On a sheet of wax paper, freezer paper or plastic wrap, form a log with the softened butter-and-herb mixture and refrigerate for at least 1 hour. This will store refrigerated for a week and frozen for longer.

Farmer's Note: Sage, parsley, mint, basil—whatever your herbs of choice—all make delicious herb butter. I happen to love rosemary and usually have this butter on hand for everything from veggies to steak!

Farmer's Note: For a quick version of my Rosemary Butter, melt butter with 1 heaping teaspoon of chopped rosemary in a small saucepan over low heat while the sweet potatoes are roasting. Remove potatoes from the oven, loosen wedges with a spatula, then transfer to a serving dish or plates. Spoon rosemary butter over them.

Honey-Lemon Olive Oil Cake

Serves 8–10

I love this cake! It is so simple and is delicious any time of year with seasonal fruit or by itself. The flavor is very clean and only ever so slightly sweet. The sweetness comes from the honey and not from any additional sweetener or sugar. Plus, this cake will keep for a few days if covered tightly or even refrigerated.

Sugar is my downfall, so I often look for recipes that require little to no sugar but get their flavor and sweetness from other natural sugars. I often make this cake as the dessert choice or as a side dessert to offer those who wish for something sweet but not sugary. A side dessert . . . who am I kidding? I'll have both desserts any day!

3 eggs	2 tablespoons fresh lemon juice
1½ cups plain yogurt (not low-fat)	2½ cups all-purpose flour
⅔ cup olive oil	2½ teaspoons baking powder
1 cup honey	¾ teaspoon baking soda
1 teaspoon good vanilla	½ teaspoon salt
2 heaping tablespoons grated lemon zest (from 2 large lemons)	

Preheat oven to 350 degrees. Grease a 9-inch springform pan and line the bottom with parchment paper.

In a large bowl, whisk eggs lightly. Add yogurt, olive oil, honey, vanilla, lemon zest and juice; whisk till combined. Add remaining ingredients and whisk until just smooth and no lumps remain—but do not over-whisk.

Pour the batter into the cake pan and bake for 60-70 minutes, until a tester comes out clean (cover with foil if the top is getting too dark toward the end). Cool in the pan on a wire rack for 10 minutes; remove cake from pan and let cool completely.

This cake will stay fresh for several days, well wrapped.

Amaretto Peach Bake

Serves 8

I've seen this recipe with pears, plums and apples, but I adore this peach version, especially since the peach flavor is accented with almond liqueur. This dish is a nod back to my grandmother's generation. Many of them were temperate types of ladies, but they sure loved a good dose of amaretto! "We're not drinking liquor, we're baking with it!" many a Southern dame has proclaimed.

4	peaches, halved and pitted (peeled, if desired)		8	tablespoons (1 stick) butter
1½	cups amaretto liqueur			Whipped cream, optional
2	dozen small amaretto cookies, crushed			Mint or basil for garnish

Preheat oven to 350 degrees.

Place peaches in baking dish, pit side up. Fill each pit with a heaping tablespoon of cookies and top with 1 tablespoon of butter.

Pour amaretto around peaches, making a vat of liqueur.

Cover loosely with foil and bake for 25 to 30 minutes, or until peaches are completely soft.

Serve with whipped cream or ice cream.

Garnish with mint or basil. I love the essence the basil gives off with the warm peaches.

Farmer's Note: I like to keep the skin on because it helps hold the peaches together.

Opening Night DINNER

JTF

Opening Night Dinner

Garden Tomatoes with Watermelon & Basil

Cornmeal-Crusted Okra

with Zesty Sour Cream

Goat Cheese Tartlets

Herb-Scented Baked Chicken

Cornmeal-Dusted Catfish

Bacon-Wrapped Beef Filets

Southern Succotash Salad

Pecan Pralines

*E*ach year, the Cashiers Historical Society hosts its Designer's Showhouse to benefit said society. Thousands of visitors flock to this mountain hamlet to tour a private home-turned-showhouse, where designers from across the Southeast, and local talents too, have transformed the home and property into a destination of utmost regard. I plan my summers around this event, for I am ever so fortunate to have been a part of the showhouse for several years.

Opening night of the Designer's Showhouse is always *the* party of the summer season in Cashiers. Hundreds of guests dressed in their mountain chic cocktail attire tour the home and fill the evening with dinner and dancing. The décor itself gilds the lily, and dining amid majestic scenery is a grand part of the whole experience. After all, that's what this party is—an experience for the senses!

Food and flowers are in my line of work, but I tip my hat to some pros who know how to feed several hundred folks and set the scene beautifully as well. Kathy Rainer and Tricky Wolfes have been peas in a pod since their college days. Their company, Parties to Die For, is known across the Southeast for fabulously fantastic floral creations and settings. For events ranging from parties hosted by First Ladies to private dinners to major benefits, these gals and their team of talented craftsmen can transform any venue into a wonderland.

For the Designer's Showhouse party, Rainer and Wolfes looked to the land and garden for inspiration and ingenuity too. Boughs of greenery from the surrounding landscape along with a bevy of blossoms from the garden were arranged together in urns atop wine barrels, creating mountainous bouquets reflecting the Appalachian mountain scenery. Tables were centered with roses, zinnias, orchids, dahlias, lilies and lustrous garden greens—an enchanting mix of garden and florist flowers all arranged in delightful shades, hues and tints. When the setting itself is breathtaking, simply elegant yet totally amazing arrangements by Kathy and Tricky are truly icing on the cake!

My friend Mr. Lee Epting and his awesome army of cooks, servers, runners and simply extraordinary staff, fed the masses at this event, as is their forte! Epting Events is the Southeast's premier event planner, serving chic locales such as Cashiers and Highlands, Sea Island, Atlanta, Savannah, Charleston and a host of others towns, farms and locations in between!

Lee's events are always delicious to the eyes and taste—which, I feel, is his winning combination. From the starting appetizers to the final sweet notes of the meal, Lee's menus are Southern-based and -influenced, and, like any good bit of Southern food, always served respectfully, beautifully and delectably. From this opening night party, I was inspired to imitate—and hopefully sincerely flatter—the menu and my friend Lee, scaled down just a tad!

Food and flowers are truly passions of mine. A night of celebrating the designers, patrons and Cashiers Historical Society amid a splendid setting is nothing shy of amazing. Thank you Kathy, Tricky, Lee and all my friends in Cashiers for such a wonderful party—I cannot wait for our next soirée!

Garden Tomatoes with Watermelon and Basil

Southern summertime classics all combined and served as a flavorful salad. The colors are as intense as the flavor!

Tomatoes, cut into wedges

Watermelon, cut same size as tomatoes

Sea salt

Basil, julienned

Olive oil, optional

Slice up wedges of garden-fresh tomatoes and watermelon and sprinkle with salt and pepper and julienned basil. An ever so slight drizzle of olive oil doesn't hurt either!

Cornmeal-Crusted Okra with Zesty Sour Cream

Serves 4–6

Okra is one of my absolute favorite summer crops. Fried, roasted, pickled or stewed—I can lap up a mess of okra anytime it is served. This version of "fried" okra takes the fear of frying out of the equation and lessens the calories, too. An oven "fry," in this case, still gives a nice flavor that is enhanced with the caramelization caused by this gentle roasting. Anything fried or roasted and served with a dipping sauce is a winner, to me!

2 dozen okra pods, sliced lengthwise	¾ cup cornmeal, yellow or white
½ cup olive or pecan oil	2 tablespoons freshly grated Parmesan cheese
Salt and pepper	

Preheat oven to 400 degrees.

Arrange the sliced okra on a greased baking sheet. Drizzle with oil and season to taste with salt and pepper. Roast for 10 minutes, or until pods start to brown.

Mix the cornmeal and Parmesan together. Remove okra from oven and sprinkle generously with the cornmeal mixture. Return to the oven for further browning and roasting, about 3 to 5 minutes more.

Farmer's Note: Alternatively, try this quick-fry method. Cut the okra into rounds and fry it in a skillet with some oil. Once the okra begins to become tender and brown, mix in the cornmeal, salt and pepper, stir and serve!

ZESTY SOUR CREAM

Makes about 1¾ cups

1 cup sour cream	1 tablespoon grated onion
½ cup mayonnaise	1 tablespoon minced chives
1 teaspoon lemon juice	¼ teaspoon curry powder
¼ teaspoon salt	½ teaspoon Worcestershire sauce
¼ teaspoon paprika	1 clove garlic, minced
¼ cup minced parsley or chervil	1 tablespoon capers with a touch of liquid

Combine all ingredients well. Stores for up to a week in the refrigerator. Yummy for sandwiches too!

Goat Cheese Tartlets

Serves 6–8

The Deep South is so fortunate to have amazing cheese makers, such as Sweet Grass Dairy in Thomasville, Georgia, and Belle Chevre in Elkmont, Alabama. From theses artisans, an explosion of fabulous flavor has become readily available for our tables. I find myself inventing ways to incorporate these awesome cheeses and products into menus and dishes. My friend Tasia Malakasis's story with Belle Chevre is nothing short of awe-inspiring.

Georgia now has a premier olive oil farm down in Lakeland. Georgia Olive Farms, run by buddy Jason Shaw, is growing and producing some of the best olive oil right smack in the Peach State. In fact, Georgia Olive Farms has produced the first commercial harvest of olive oil east of the Mississippi River since the 19th century! Their olive oil has become a staple in my kitchen; the flavor and texture are luscious and smooth.

For this dish, I combine flavors from across the Deep South. I love the flavor of goat cheese and onion—the tango of tangy and sweet with a touch of tartness. The combination of flavors is perfect as a spread or starter itself but ideal as a filler for an omelet, a pizza or burger topping, a salad addition, a steak side or a chicken, pork or fish accompaniment. From French-style Alabama goat cheese to olive oil and onions from Georgia, this dish is full of flavor—and pride for my fellow Southerners.

1 tablespoon butter	2 tablespoons balsamic vinegar
2 Vidalia onions, sliced into strips	8 ounces Belle Chevre goat cheese
1 medium red onion, sliced into strips	Cornbread crisps, toasted biscuit halves, crackers, naan, or ginger snaps
½ teaspoon of salt	
½ teaspoon pepper	Sea salt
2 tablespoons Georgia Olive Oil	Chives or other herbs, minced, for garnish

Over low heat, melt the butter and add the sliced onions. Season with salt and pepper, drizzle with the olive oil and vinegar, and then cover so the onions can slowly sweat. Gently toss the onions frequently; they should brown and caramelize but not burn. This takes 15 to 20 minutes or longer, depending on how browned and caramelized you like your onions and how low and slow you are cooking. This creates a sweet onion jam.

Spread Belle Chevre over your cracker of choice and top with the onion jam. Garnish with sprinkles of sea salt, chives or other minced herbs.

Herb-Scented Baked Chicken

Serves 6

This is my "Scarborough Fair" recipe for chicken. Parsley, sage, rosemary and thyme all make their way into this dish, and during baking the combination makes the whole house smell divine! I use this herb mix with some salts and other seasonings and like to keep it on hand. It is wonderful for roasting a whole hen or baking individual pieces of chicken.

These herbs all grow well throughout the year for us in the South, but the autumn and winter months are especially enchanting times for these flavors. Sage is often paired with poultry, while rosemary and thyme are evergreen for the Deep South. Parsley thrives in our warm falls and mild winters and bolts in the springtime. I prefer using these herbs fresh from the garden, and when doing so, the quantity is more; their flavor intensifies when they are dried. Try now to make this dish and not have "Scarborough Fair" stuck in your mind for the rest of the day!

1 small (5- to 6-pound) roasting hen, giblets removed,* or 6 medium chicken breasts, boneless or bone-in

½ cup roughly chopped parsley, flat or curly leaf, or ¼ cup dried

2 tablespoons roughly chopped sage, or 1 tablespoon dried

¼ cup roughly chopped rosemary, or 2 tablespoons dried

2 tablespoons thyme leaves, no stems, or 1 tablespoon dried**

1 tablespoon course sea salt

1 teaspoon garlic salt

½ tablespoon cracked black pepper

1 tablespoon melted butter, optional

¼ cup olive oil

Pat the chicken dry with paper towels.

Combine herbs with salts and pepper. A splash of melted butter helps bring them together if so desired.

Coat the whole hen or chicken breasts with olive oil and generously sprinkle with the herb mixture (inside and out for a whole hen, both sides for breasts).

For chicken breasts, preheat oven to 350 degrees and bake 15 to 20 minutes for boneless chicken breasts, 30 to 40 minutes for bone-in breasts.

For roasting a 5- to 6-pound bird, I roast at 425 degrees for about 1 hour and 20 minutes covered, then for 10 minutes at 450 degrees uncovered to brown the skin. Check the weight of your bird and follow the packager's recommended time allotment for its poundage. Cook it until the juices run clear when a knife is inserted between the thigh and leg. When done, allow chicken to rest for about 15 to 20 minutes before carving. Slice dark and white meat pieces for serving.

*If roasting a hen, be sure to add some onions inside the cavity and other root veggies in and around for a complete meal and more flavor. The giblets can be used to make gravy, with chicken stock, veggies, seasoning and boiled egg.

**Lemon thyme is delicious!

Cornmeal-Dusted Catfish

Serves 6

"Winner, winner! Catfish Dinner!" Catfish is a major agricultural item for the Deep South. Whether we're frying it at tailgates or fish fries proper, this foodstuff is as much a part of our culinary heritage as grits, biscuits and cornbread! For my birthday, my family or a group of friends trek down to Daphne Lodge outside Cordele, Georgia, for catfish and steak. I love the history and heritage of this restaurant. Hardly another place holds such happy memories of good food, family time and fellowship.

Frying up a mess of catfish can be a chore, and I know I couldn't outdo Daphne's. So this recipe is my version of fried catfish and may be a bit healthier, too, since it is baked. Of course, you can fry it if you'd like, but once you've tasted this version, you might just put your oil to rest!

6 whole catfish filets or 12 catfish "fingers" or strips, washed and patted dry	¾ cup panko or crumbled Ritz crackers
2 heaping cups buttermilk	1 teaspoon seasoned salt
1½ cups cornmeal	½ teaspoon salt
	½ teaspoon pepper
	Paprika

Soak catfish in buttermilk for 15 to 20 minutes.

Preheat oven to 350 degrees.

You'll need two baking sheets—one greased and one ungreased. On the ungreased baking sheet, mix the cornmeal, crumbs, salts and pepper. Dredge the catfish, coating both sides amply. Lay the coated filets on the greased baking sheet.

Bake the filets for 15 to 20 minutes, until golden brown and the fish flakes with a fork. Dust with paprika. Serve with Mere's Tartar Sauce.

Farmer's Note: For a bit of *South by Southwest* flavor, add 1 teaspoon cumin and ¾ teaspoon chili powder to the dredging. Some smoked paprika adds nice color too.

MERE'S TARTAR SAUCE

Makes about 1 cup

My baby sister, Meredith, was the pickiest eater of our brood. Yet she loved tartar sauce, a side Maggie and I could take or leave. The peculiar thing about this is that Mere does not like mayonnaise. (If she does not see it used, we can sneak it into a sauce or dip. Shhh . . . don't tell her! The secret's in the sauce!)

1 cup mayonnaise

Juice of 2 lemon wedges

1 heaping tablespoon capers
  with a splash of their liquid

1 tablespoon sweet relish

1 tablespoon grated onion

½ teaspoon salt

½ teaspoon pepper

Mix everything together and serve with fried fish. Also great with shrimp or on po' boys!

Farmer's Note: The big difference between Southern-style tartar sauce and others is that we typically use a sweet pickle rather than a gherkin or cornichons since the capers provide the savory bite already. Totally a taste preference, y'all.

Bacon-Wrapped Beef Filets

Serves 6

This is a dish where knowing your butcher is a plus! Not only will he cut the perfect-size filet from the tenderloin but he'll wrap it, too—with bacon! For this particular filet, I like an almost medallion-sized cut. It cooks ever so quickly on the grill or in an iron skillet. This cut also makes a great choice for a buffet, since a large beef tenderloin sliced into medallions can yield a gracious plenty.

I'm a firm believer that delicious beef needs very little seasoning. My fair state boasts some amazing cattle farms and beef purveyors, including my friends in Bluffton, Georgia, at White Oak Pastures. One can literally taste the difference in their grass-fed beef and other products, such as grass-fed lamb, free-range poultry and pastured eggs.

A simple marinade is all this delicious beef needs—if that. I love to grill over oak and hickory wood or use an iron skillet on the stove to form a great crust and then finish the filet in the oven.

½ cup soy sauce	Salt and pepper	
½ cup Worcestershire sauce	6 small pats butter, room temperature	
6 bacon-wrapped filets		

Whisk soy and Worcestershire sauces together and marinate the filets for at least 30 minutes or up to overnight.

Remove filets from marinade and sprinkle salt and pepper on both sides.

Preheat oven to 400 degrees if you want the filets to be more done than medium-rare.

In a lightly greased and heated iron skillet, brown top and bottom sides of the filets for up to 2 minutes, depending on how thick the filet is cut. The salt and pepper and the skillet's heat will form a crust and start crisping the bacon too! Place a pat of butter on each filet and then tent with foil. The filets will be a good medium-rare after browning. To cook further, transfer skillet with filets to the preheated oven and finish cooking to desired doneness.

Southern Succotash Salad

Serves 4–6

My friends at Stripling's General Store carry a wide assortment of Southern foodstuffs, from butchered meats to sausages, sauces and snacks, groceries and produce to dressings and specialty items. One such item I love to use in salads and other dishes is their Vidalia Onion Cracked Peppercorn Dressing, especially on my take of their succotash salad.

1 (16-ounce) bag fresh or frozen lima beans

3 cups fresh or frozen corn kernels

3 teaspoons butter

1 cup cherry tomatoes, halved (I like to mix yellow and red)

1 cup chopped red onion

2 teaspoons chopped fresh thyme, more for garnish

¼ cup buttermilk

2 tablespoons milk

6 ounces Stripling's Vidalia Onion Cracked Peppercorn Dressing*

Salt

Chopped chives, optional garnish

Julienned basil, optional garnish

Boil lima beans and corn over medium-high heat until tender; then drain. Add butter, tomatoes, onion, thyme, and milks. Cook for another 15 minutes. Remove from direct heat and allow to cool to room temperature. Stir in dressing and salt to taste. Garnish with thyme, chopped chives or julienned basil.

One (12-ounce) bottle of Stripling's Vidalia Onion Cracked Peppercorn Dressing will meet the recipe requirement and leave a nice amount remaining for other uses.

Pecan Pralines

Makes about 3 dozen

This is going to stir up a debate across the South.

Mr. Lee Epting makes the best pecan pralines I've ever had. Lee and his team make pralines by the thousands every year for their events. They are sweet but not too sweet. Giant copper pots are used for the making, and then they are served from amazingly handsome platters and trays, along with complementary side offerings such as a balsamic vinegar reduction and ice cream.

I pronounce this delicacy as "pray—lean" while folks all across Dixieland pronounce it in a varying number of ways, which will further stir up the debate. The debate, y'all, is that I may think Lee's are the best, but someone's grandmother or aunt somewhere else makes the best, to them. Let me just state for the record that if I need to be nominated as official praline taster for the South, I gladly accept!

Furthermore, a debate may rage in the name itself. Some folks say that "pecan pralines" is redundant. In most of the South, "pralines" mean pecan pralines—end of story. Anyways, I still do not mind being official praline tester for the South.

This is my feeble attempt at imitating the master! Many other recipes abound, but this one is simple enough for me.

1 pound light brown sugar	1 tablespoon butter
¾ cup evaporated milk	½ teaspoon vanilla
⅛ teaspoon salt	2 cups toasted pecans broken into bits

In a medium-size pot over low heat, mix and cook the sugar, milk, salt, butter and vanilla together until the sugar dissolves.

Add pecans and cook over medium heat, stirring constantly, until the mixture reaches the soft-ball stage.

Remove from heat and continue stirring for 5 minutes, while the mixture cools. Stir rapidly until the mixture thickens and coats the pecans.

Rapidly drop spoonfuls onto tinfoil or wax paper, forming patties. If the candy is too thick to drop and form a patty, add a few drops of hot water. Spoon size will determine patty size—I use a tablespoon.

Allow the patties to set and cool.

Farmer's Notes: Candy making in the South can depend on the weather. Unlike divinity, pralines can be made whatever the weather.

Toasting and even slightly salting the pecans makes all the difference in this recipe. I cannot get enough of the sweet-salty singsong combination!

Laura Lyn   Brince

Rehearsal Dinner ON THE Grounds

JTF

Rehearsal Dinner
on the grounds

Baked Chicken with Peach Glaze

Spinach Salad with Berries & Feta Cheese
& Honey-Lemon Vinaigrette

Pimiento Cheese Mini Sandwiches

French Green Beans

Tortellini Salad with Artichokes, Tomatoes & Olives

Open-Faced Cucumber Sandwiches

Gazpacho Shooters

Watermelon Ice

Sour Cream Biscuits

Orange Sorbet with Baboo's Tea Cake

Mama Doris's Banana Pudding with Kahlua

*W*eddings and their surrounding festivities are such wonderful times to celebrate with your closest friends and family. Often a wedding guest is a guest proper of either the groom or the bride. As for this wedding, both are near and dear to me.

The groom, Mr. Brince Coody, is a childhood friend and younger brother of my lifelong and dearest friend, Maggie Coody Griffin. The bride, the now Mrs. Brince Coody and formerly Miss Laura Lyn McLeod, just happens to be my office manager and, as I have dubbed her, "my boss." She wears many hats at my company, from design associate to event planner—and I could not be any more grateful for her dedication and amazing work ethic. Hardly a better match could have ever happened!

Their courtship, engagement and wedding were nothing short of a fairytale. From sisters and cousins arranging their meeting to the wedding day full of all the wonderful accoutrements one can imagine, this couple's magnetism is simply inspiring, encouraging and full of prospect.

As is the groom's family's duty, a rehearsal dinner is set the night before the wedding day. Brince's family's home in Hawkinsville proved to be the ideal setting for this prenuptial meal. Tucked onto a gentle rise amid a glade of pines and oaks, the Coody home was the perfect setting for the dinner. This home, special to Brince, of course, as his childhood home, is special to so many others too—for not only did the Coody children grow up in this house, but so did all of their friends. Hardly another home besides my own is filled with so many memories of childhood, high school days, home from college times, and milestone events in our adult lives. Events such as Brince and Laura Lyn's rehearsal dinner here are all too apropos and fitting, for us all.

Brince's parents did something very unique. They befriended us—the friends of their children, thus making their home even more special. Whether it is for business advice, a chance to catch up or a rehearsal dinner, any night spent with this family is a treasured time, especially when the dinner involves their family recipes!

From childhood to adulthood faves, the rehearsal dinner menu reflected Brince's tastes and heritage. Even the desserts were from Baboo and Mama Doris—the grandmothers who also loved and nurtured their children and grandchildren and their friends. I don't rank many ladies as high as "Mimi status," but Baboo and Mama Doris make the cut! Kicking off a weekend of two fine families joining one another made this rehearsal dinner on these familial grounds truly memorable.

Baked Chicken with Peach Glaze

Serves 4

We Georgians find a way to use peaches anytime! Peach preserves are a mainstay for Southern cooks, for we can marinate, bake, baste and top nearly every course of our meals with them. Preserves, as opposed to jelly, are chock-full of bits of the fruit itself, thus delivering a stronger flavor. These preserves along with the mildness of shallots are perfect atop any piece of chicken!

4   boneless, skinless chicken breasts

Juice of 1 lemon (Meyer preferred)

Kosher salt and freshly ground black pepper

1   shallot, minced

2   cloves garlic, minced

1   cup peach preserves

Preheat oven to 400 degrees.

Place chicken in a lightly greased baking dish. Squeeze the juice of 1 lemon over the chicken and season to taste with salt and pepper.

In a small bowl, mix together the shallot, garlic, and peach preserves. Spoon mixture over the chicken. Bake uncovered for 1 hour.

Farmer's Note: Browning the chicken breasts first in an iron skillet with some butter or olive oil creates a wonderful depth of flavor. Then topping them with the onions and preserves, baking until done, makes a glaze on the chicken and can cut down on the total baking time a little.

Spinach Salad with Berries and Feta Cheese

Serves 4

This simple salad pairs well with so many dishes. When different berries come into season, their flavors can enhance the salad. Mixing berries is yummy too!

4 cups baby spinach leaves	¾ cup walnuts
½ cup fresh berries	Honey-Lemon Vinaigrette (see below)
⅓ cup crumbled feta cheese	

Toss ingredients in a large serving bowl. Top with Honey-Lemon Vinaigrette.

HONEY-LEMON VINAIGRETTE

Zest of ½ lemon	1 tablespoon honey
Juice of 2 lemons	Pinch of salt and pepper
3 tablespoons olive oil	

Whisk all ingredients well in a small bowl or container.

Pimento Cheese Mini Sandwiches

Makes about 2½ cups

Whether you are getting married or buried—whatever the event—we Southerners serve pimento cheese. From our grits in the morning to a topper for burgers or just a snack with crackers, having pimento cheese on hand is paramount in a Southern kitchen.

Mimi always told me that "if you serve it crustless and on a silver platter, it is fancy." Southern culture is not pretentious—it is a celebration of life's every moments. Pimento cheese is thus on hand for each and every celebration.

1 cup finely shredded sharp cheddar cheese*	Squirt of lemon juice
1 cup finely shredded sharp Vermont white cheddar cheese*	Dash of Lawry's Seasoned Salt
	Dash of Morton Nature's Seasons
½–¾ cup mayonnaise (your preference)	Pinch of cayenne pepper
½ jar Lindsay's pimento pieces with some juice	Cracked black pepper
	Cracked sea salt
	White bread

Place all ingredients except bread together in a medium-size bowl and stir until well blended. Serve on white bread and top with another slice of bread. Remove the crust and cut into fours.

The already shredded is fine, but shredding your own really does make a difference.

BL
08.23.13

Hors d'oeuvres
Open Faced Cucumber Sandwiches
Pimiento Cheese Mini Sandwiches
Gazpacho Shooters
Salad Watermelon Ice
Spinach Salad with Strawberries, Feta, & Walnuts
Olive Oil & Honey Vinaigrette

Entree
Baked Chicken Breast with Peach Glaze
Pasta Salad with Tomatoes, Artichokes & Olives
French Green Beans and Sour Cream Biscuit
Dessert
Orange Sorbet with Baboo's Tea Cake
Mama Doris Banana Pudding with Kahlua

French Green Beans

Serves 4

A recipe like this is filled with memories of dinners and events where I've tasted and feasted on this dish, but also memories of the lessons learned from preparing it. I can hear the words of Mimi or Mrs. Mary, or Baboo or Susie or any of the great ladies who have inspired me and taught me so much about cooking, Southern style and life in general. I leave their words in the instructions, to teach us about blanching and shocking. Cherished culinary lessons indeed; yet, it is the times spent in the kitchen with such beloved women that amount to some of my life's greatest treasures.

1 pound fresh green beans	¼ cup unseasoned breadcrumbs**
2 tablespoons fresh duck fat or bacon drippings*	Salt and freshly ground pepper
	Grated Parmesan or Romano cheese

Snap off the stem ends of the beans. Boil a large pot of water, about 4 quarts. Fill a bowl about the same time with ice water and set it aside.

When the water is boiling briskly, boil the beans for about 3 minutes. Do not cook them all the way. This is called blanching. Drain them in a colander and plunge them into the ice water. This is called shocking and it helps preserve the bright green color. Drain and pat dry as possible with paper towels. You can do this a day or two in advance.

Heat the duck fat or bacon drippings in a frying pan over a medium to medium-high flame. Add the beans and toss them around so they brown a bit on all sides, but don't let them scorch. This should take about 5 minutes.

Turn the heat down to medium and add the breadcrumbs. Toss until they coat the beans and let them toast.

Turn the heat down to low. Add salt and pepper to taste. Don't waste any of the breadcrumbs that fell off the beans into the pan. Sprinkle them over the beans.

Just before serving, sprinkle the beans generously with Parmesan or Romano cheese after plating, or serve the cheese on the side and let your guests sprinkle it on their plates.

Butter will work if you don't have duck fat or bacon drippings.

You can use seasoned breadcrumbs if you wish.

Tortellini Salad with Artichokes, Tomatoes and Olives

Serves 4

Maybe it is their name. Maybe it is because they share the same tastes as their grandmothers. Maybe it is from their forays through Italy. Whatever the reason, both my sister and my best friend Maggie love this salad, and so it reminds me of them. Mimi and Baboo both loved this salad and these flavors too. I think taste palates are hereditary. Being the thoughtful grandmothers they were, they would cater to our likes and dislikes. Thus, since I do not relish olives like these girls do, my share went to them—and still does!

¼   cup white wine vinegar

1   teaspoon salt

½   teaspoon freshly ground pepper

1   tablespoon honey

½   cup olive oil

⅓   cup chopped flat-leaf parsley

1   cup cherry tomatoes

½   cup olives (green, black, mixed, your choice)

1   (14-ounce) can artichokes in water

1   (9-ounce) package refrigerated Bertolli cheese tortellini

Mix together the vinegar, salt, pepper, and honey in a large bowl. Slowly whisk in the olive oil.

Toss the parsley, tomatoes, olives, and artichokes in the dressing.

Cook the tortellini according to the package directions. Drain and cool with cold water. Gently toss with the rest of the ingredients. Chill in the fridge until you are ready to serve.

Open-Faced Cucumber Sandwiches

Makes 30–40 sandwiches

Back to Mimi's adage of sans crust and silver platters, this dish is a Southern hallmark for entertaining. Plus, when our gardens have gifted us with cucumbers aplenty, this is a great way to feed the masses with their bounty.

1 loaf white sandwich bread	¼ teaspoon pepper
½ cup (4 ounces) cream cheese	1 tablespoon finely chopped fresh dill, plus more for garnish
¼ teaspoon garlic powder	
¼ teaspoon salt	1 seedless cucumber, sliced thinly into rounds

To prepare bread, roll each slice with a rolling pin to flatten slightly, then use a round cutter to cut bread into small circles (you should get two circles from each slice). Cover with a damp paper towel to keep from drying out.

Mix cream cheese, garlic powder, salt, pepper and 1 tablespoon dill in a small bowl. Spread lightly on bread, top with cucumbers and garnish with fresh dill sprigs. Cover with a damp paper towel until ready to serve.

Gazpacho Shooters

Makes about 4½ cups

The Piedmont Driving Club is an institution in Atlanta. It still retains the traditions of the Old South yet is poised and avant-garde enough for the New South. Growing up, if we were invited to the PDC, that meant wearing our Sunday best—and acting it, too!

I can remember the first time I ever had a cold soup—a "purposely served cold" soup. It was the famous creamy leek and potato gazpacho at the Piedmont Driving Club, and I have loved it ever since. Sure, it is delicious served warm, but when the heat is blazing in the South come summertime, anything cold is welcome refreshment.

I can vividly remember Mama's glance toward me that day at the PDC. Her eyes can tell a story, give a command, stop an action or soothe any ache in a flash. Before I could even say, "Mama, my soup is COLD!" she intercepted my acclamation with that flashing glance, and said, "This gazpacho is delicious. Mmmm."

I knew then that the cold soup was purposely served to our table, and that the dish had a fancy name, too. I was enthralled! Now whenever I'm entertaining a crowd al fresco, gazpacho is a fun choice. Any chance to chill a delicious soup and serve it to my guests as a "shooter" is an additional bit of fun!

3 large tomatoes, quartered and seeded	2 cups vegetable juice
1 jalapeño pepper, minced	1 cucumber, chopped, for garnish (cocktail shrimp, pickled okra, pickled baby corn or black pepper can be used)
3 tablespoons lemon juice	
1½ teaspoons salt	

Combine tomatoes, jalapeño pepper, lemon juice and salt in a blender. Pulse until it is well blended but not smooth. You want it to be a little chunky. Pour the mixture into a bowl and add the vegetable juice. Stir well, then cover and chill before serving. It does separate so will need another good stir right before serving. Use shot glasses or single-serve containers for plating. Once you have plated the gazpacho, top the servings with your choice of garnish.

Watermelon Ice

Serves roughly 10–12

How chic is this dish? The trade-off for summer's heat is its produce. Watermelon is a major crop for many farming families in our area, including Laura Lyn's. Thus, totally apropos to serve this at her rehearsal dinner.

The color of watermelon ice is remarkable, and the very essence is attractive and elegant. From the first spoonful to the last gulp (you'll be drinking it if served outside), you'll delight in what the Italians call a *semifreddo,* or semi-frozen dish. Or as we Southerners say, "It is just good, y'all!" Enjoy.

5-6 cups watermelon chunks	1 tablespoon watermelon liqueur (if you are making this for children, double the lemon juice and omit liqueur)
¼ cup sugar (decrease or omit if the watermelon is really sweet)	
1 tablespoon lemon juice	Mint, optional
	Lemon rind strips, optional

Scrape the inside out of a watermelon, discarding the seeds, and place fruit in the blender with sugar, if using, lemon juice and watermelon liqueur. Blend on high. You may have to do this in several batches to ensure your kitchen walls and cabinets stay clean!

Squeeze the juice through a fine sieve and pour into a large, shallow metal pan. You can use a glass pan, but metal helps in the formation of ice crystals.

Freeze the mixture and mix with a fork every 30 minutes to form ice crystals. Continue this for 2 to 3 hours, until the entire pan is filled with watermelon ice.

Garnish with mint or lemon rind strips and serve in small cocktail glasses or footed ice cream glasses.

Sour Cream Biscuits

Makes a gracious dozen small biscuits

The Swanson House in downtown Perry serves these biscuits. My office happens to be across the street and so these biscuits are a part of our lunches more often than not. Sour Cream Biscuits of this nomenclature are widely served throughout the South. Taste one and you'll know why!

What I tell people about these biscuits is this: if you cannot make a buttermilk biscuit from scratch, then make these. Though the two are not the same, they are very similar in taste. Perfect on their own or gilded with a fruit jelly, preserve or even apple butter, these biscuits won't last for long!

2   cups self-rising flour

1   cup (2 sticks) butter, room temperature

1   cup sour cream

Preheat the oven to 400 degrees. Grease miniature muffin pans.

Mix the flour and butter together, add the sour cream, and blend well. Spoon the batter into the muffin pans. Bake until golden, 8 to 10 minutes.

Orange Sorbet with Baboo's Tea Cakes

Serves 6

I included Baboo's Tea Cakes in my book *Sip and Savor*, for they are a delectable accompaniment to many drinks. A delectable accompaniment to many desserts, too! A bond I have found among friends throughout my childhood and now into adulthood is that special, most precious bond between a grandchild and grandmother. When I meet someone whose life has been nurtured, shaped and guided by his or her beloved grandmother, then I know this person is a friend to cherish and bond with. That's a bond the Coody and Farmer children have shared throughout our childhood and into our lives today.

Mrs. Barbara, affectionately known as "Baboo" by her grandchildren (and her grandchildren's friends), truly embodied grace and elegance. Her style was legendary and her taste flawless.

This is a dessert that I could have over and over and never tire of! I love the creamy citrus flavor of the sorbet and the crunchy sweetness from the tea cakes.

8 ounces (2 sticks) butter, softened	1 egg, beaten
1½ cups sugar	1 teaspoon vanilla
2½ cups self-rising flour	

Preheat oven to 350 degrees. Grease a baking sheet.

With a mixer, beat the butter and then add the sugar and beat well. Add flour slowly, mixing with butter and sugar between additions. Fold in the egg and vanilla until incorporated. Refrigerate dough for 30 minutes. Shape into 1½-inch balls (or roll out and use cookie cutters). Place on prepared baking sheet and bake for 10 to 15 minutes, or until edges are golden.

Farmer's Note: These also make the perfect "bread" for ice cream sandwiches.

ORANGE SORBET

Makes about 1¼ quarts

1 cup sugar	3 cups orange juice
1 cup water	3 tablespoons lemon juice
12 strips of orange peel (1 to 3 inches long)	2 tablespoons orange liqueur or vodka

In a small saucepan, bring the sugar, water and orange peel to a boil. Cook and stir until sugar is dissolved; discard orange peel. Set aside to cool.

In a large bowl, combine the orange juice, lemon juice, orange liqueur and reserved sugar mixture. Fill the cylinder of an ice cream freezer, and freeze according to manufacturer's directions.

Transfer to a freezer container; freeze for 8 hours or overnight.

Farmer's Note: Lemon or lime sorbet can be made in the same fashion. Just substitute the orange peel, juice and liqueur for those of the fruit being used.

Mama Doris's Banana Pudding with Kahlua

Serves 8–10

Mama Doris was the Coody children's paternal grandmother—as fine a lady as could be. I remember how she made everyone feel as welcome in her home as if you were her own kin. A farmer's wife, Mama Doris knew how to feed a crowd of hungry farmers and her family too. Her heart and home were warm reflections of her affectionate nature and lovely spirit.

A classically Southern lady, Mama Doris cooked like many Southern women—she simply cooked! Recipes proper served as inspirations and, as my Mimi said, "mere suggestions" as to how things were to go whilst cooking.

Banana pudding is a Southern dessert of legendary lore. Some Southern cooks want the ripest of ripe bananas and others want them green. Some make custard while others call it a pudding proper, where you use a pudding mix or simply make boiled custard. Do you fold the whipped cream into the pudding or do you serve it on the side or as a sub layer of the meringue?

Regardless of the procedure, the end result is a dessert as sweet and memorable as the cooks themselves. Here's to grandmothers like Mama Doris, who fed their broods physically but also nurtured our minds and spirits just as devotedly!

2	small (3.4-ounce) packages vanilla pudding mix		1	cup whipping cream
3¾	cups sweet milk		2	dozen vanilla wafers
3	eggs, separated		4–6	bananas sliced into thin rounds (depending on how much banana you prefer)
⅓	cup Kahlua*		⅓	cup sugar
3	teaspoons vanilla, divided			

In a medium saucepan over medium heat, gradually blend the pudding mix and milk.

Beat the egg yolks (the whites are for the meringue) with 1 teaspoon vanilla and slowly add them to the milk and pudding mix, tempering the yolks first with a bit of the warm milk.

Add the Kahlua to the pudding, stirring constantly until it reaches a full boil, then remove from the heat. Cover the pudding with plastic wrap that touches the top of the pudding so as to prevent a skin from forming. Allow to cool thoroughly, about 25 minutes.

While the pudding is cooling, whip the cream and remaining 2 teaspoons vanilla together until soft peaks form. Fold the whipped cream into the cooled pudding.* (See Farmer's Note.)

In a casserole or glass serving dish, arrange vanilla wafers to cover the bottom of the dish. Spoon half the pudding over the wafers and top the pudding with sliced banana. Repeat the layers once more. Some folks prefer the banana layer atop the wafers; to each his own.

Preheat oven to 350 degrees.

Beat the egg whites, gradually adding the sugar, until stiff peaks form. Spoon meringue over cooled pudding and bananas and bake until meringue is lightly browned, about 7 to 8 minutes.

A bit of Kahlua can be added to the whipped cream (about a teaspoon or so) for further flavor. Also, a homemade Kahlua can be made if none is on hand or obtainable.

Farmer's Note: If making in a trifle dish for presentation, then layer the pudding and whipped cream if desired. You may need to double your whipped cream if doing so.

HOMEMADE KAHLUA

Makes about 7 cups

1	quart water	3	tablespoons instant coffee granules or 1 cup strongly brewed hot coffee
2	cups sugar (if you like it sweeter, then another ¼–½ cup is fine)	1	tablespoon vanilla
		2½	cups vodka

In a medium saucepan, bring water, sugar and coffee to a boil. Turn down heat and simmer slowly—very slowly—for about 3 hours. The mixture will be very dark and syrupy. Allow the mixture to cool; then add the vanilla and vodka.

Farmer's Note: I like to keep some on hand for ladling over ice cream or pouring into bottles or Mason jars for gifts.

Wedding Reception

Menu

Hors D'oeuvres   Mac n' Cheese Balls
Bacon Wrapped Quail   Melon Caprese

Collard Green Wontons

Dinner   Pork Tenderloin

                        Shrimp n' Grits
                        Fried Green Tomatoes

                        Countryside Pasta
                        Grilled Vegetables

Dessert   cake & cobbler

Please highlight your favorite verse & sign your NAME next to it. ♡ Thanks

ON THE GROUNDS

L&B

welcome

DRINKS
are outside.

DINNER
will be served once the love birds arrive.

DANCING
will commence when the band starts its tune.

DESSERT
will be cake and peach cobbler, so make sure you save room.

PLEASE
have a really good time and don't forget to sign the guest book.

JTF

Wedding Reception

Fried Mac and Cheese Balls
Watermelon Caprese Stacks
Bacon-Wrapped Quail
Collard Green Wontons
Pork Tenderloin with Teriyaki Apricot Sauce
Summer Salad with Goat Cheese & Berries
Raspberry Balsamic Vinaigrette
Grits with Assorted Toppings
Fried Green Tomatoes
Peach Cobbler

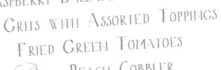

*A*fter a night of toasts comes a day of celebrating! Brince and Laura Lyn's wedding day was magical and delightful in every aspect. The South Georgia summertime temperatures even dipped and created a night of purely pleasant temps.

For the ceremony, Laura Lyn chose her home church in Cordele. This domed sanctuary is stunningly beautiful (as was the bride) on its own. Simple arrangements of hydrangeas, garden greenery and David Austin roses filled the altar and set the backdrop for the wedding ceremony.

For the reception, Laura Lyn chose a venue close to her family's farm in Pineview and quite reminiscent of herself, I must say—a modern gal with classic taste and a strong tie to her heritage. A new barn built on an antebellum farm was the setting for the wedding reception. As an event planner and designer with my firm, Laura Lyn's vision for her reception was spot-on with her style and heritage on these Georgia farmlands. From the menus painted on farm pallets to a stacked tower of cast-iron crockery, every inch of this event reflected Laura Lyn's eye for detail and paid homage to Southern hospitality.

Feeding a group such as this is no easy task. Laura Lyn chose a menu that kept its roots in Southern culinary legend and added a twist or two for modern flair; but a menu that nonetheless fed every soul in attendance and sent people back to the buffets for more! She even nodded to Brince's passion for hunting with a quail dish.

To accommodate the three hundred plus attendees, tables were scattered throughout the barn and outside the barn doors leading toward the pole tent that housed the band. Surrounded by thousands of acres of longleaf pine, hay fields and row crops, this barn is a beacon of bucolic beauty. I cannot help but feel that barns are symbolic of Southern entertaining—rooted in the land and farms, multitasked for multipurpose events, traditional in design but modern enough for today and, as is often the case, the largest open structures on our grounds capable of hosting hundreds of people.

Lanterns of every shape and size lined walkways, served as centerpieces, or hung from posts and cast their romantic glow across the reception. Floral arrangements of hydrangeas, Agarista, eucalyptus, dahlias, garden roses and magnolias heralded their splendor, from the barn's entry to the tabletops to the food buffets and cake display.

Fun and fellowship were contagious on this night. The band kept folks dancing, the food kept folks fed, and the friendships grew ever more deep. A wedding reception on the grounds—a celebration of Southern style, tradition and panache culminating into a night of memories and the best way to begin a life as husband and wife. All the very best wishes to Mr. and Mrs. Brince Coody!

Fried Mac and Cheese Balls

Makes about 3 dozen

Make your favorite "from scratch" macaroni and cheese in a shallow pan and refrigerate until cold, at least 2 hours. You can also use leftover macaroni and cheese, providing there is any! Mema's Macaroni and Cheese (see page 38) yields about 3 dozen balls.

6 cups macaroni and cheese, or whatever is left over	2 cups breadcrumbs, panko or crumbled crackers
4 eggs	4–6 cups canola or peanut oil for frying
1 tablespoon milk	

Shape the cold macaroni and cheese into meatball-sized rounds and place them on a wax paper-lined tray. Freeze overnight.

Make an egg wash by whisking the eggs and milk together in a shallow bowl. This is your "wet."

Then place the breadcrumbs in another shallow bowl. This is your "dry." You'll always have a wet and dry when frying Southern style.

Dip macaroni balls into the egg wash and then into the breadcrumbs and return to the tray.

Fry immediately or place in freezer again until ready to fry. I find that returning to the freezer to set for a few minutes helps them hold together.

Heat about 2 inches of oil in a skillet to 350 degrees. Fry macaroni and cheese balls in small batches (6 to 8) until golden brown, about 5 minutes. Serve hot.

Watermelon Caprese Stacks

Makes 24–30 skewers

This color and flavor combination is truly memorable. I have used peaches, too, for a Georgia–style Caprese Salad, and this version with watermelon is just as Georgian as a peach!

1 large watermelon, cut into cubes or balls

2 pounds mozzarella cheese, cubed

About 100 basil leaves

Flaky sea salt

Alternate watermelon and mozzarella on bamboo skewers with a small basil leaf after each coupling of watermelon and mozzarella. Sprinkle with sea salt and serve on a beautiful platter.

Bacon-Wrapped Quail

Serves 4

Quail plantations dot the landscape across South Georgia. Coveys flock amid glades, forests and fields of sedge grass, wax myrtle, longleaf pine and live oak.

Southerners have always fancied wild game dinners, whereas the city of Thomasville, Georgia, boasts to be the South's toniest quail hunting locale. This town is nestled so far down in Southwest Georgia that Tallahassee, Florida, is the next town southward. Thomasville is very close to Bainbridge, too, from where my grandmother's family hails. Hunting is a major sport for Southern gentlemen; thus, recipes for game dishes can be found in nearly every Southern cookbook. One famed such, *Pines and Plantations,* from Thomasville, boasts a fantastic array of game dishes along with recipes and menus, too.

As for me, I like a simply grilled quail leg, wrapped in bacon. Quail legs have actually become available in Southern grocery stores now, making dishes like this possible not only after a hunt but also for special events or weekend dinners.

1	cup green pepper jelly	Salt and pepper
3	tablespoons good bourbon	8 quail legs
1	teaspoon soy sauce	4 slices bacon, cut in half
1	teaspoon Worcestershire sauce	

Mix the pepper jelly, bourbon, soy sauce, and Worcestershire sauce together in a small bowl. Set aside.

Salt and pepper the quail legs and wrap with halved bacon pieces. Grill over medium heat, turning the legs frequently to cook the bacon crisply and ensure nice grill marks. Baste with the pepper jelly mixture, or serve it on the side as a sauce.

Collard Green Wontons

Makes about 70

For the release of *A Time to Cook,* my sweet friends Paula Deen and Brandon Branch hosted a fabulous party at Mrs. Paula's home in Savannah. The music, the guests, the weather, the flowers, and of course the food, were all simply divine.

Collard Green Wontons were passed around to the guests and, I must admit, I ate more than my fair share! I think they also left an impression on Laura Lyn, for she had them served at her wedding. South by Far East, you might say, for this particular dish is a delightful blend of Southern and Asian flavors and techniques. Combing the soft greens with the crispy wontons made for a wonderful complement of textures.

Here is my take on the dish served by Mrs. Paula at the party she co-hosted for me.

1 medium Vidalia onion, diced	1 teaspoon Morton Nature's Seasons
2 ounces (½ stick) butter	1 teaspoon seasoned salt
1 tablespoon olive oil, plus more for drizzling	2 tablespoons jarred jalapeños with a bit of their liquid**
2 tablespoons minced garlic	½ large bunch collard greens (about 2 dozen leaves with ribs)
1 pound back meat*	1 (8-ounce) package cream cheese, softened
4 cups chicken stock	
2 cups water	About 70 wonton wrappers
1 ½-pound ham hock	Peanut oil

In a large Dutch oven or a heavy-bottomed pot, brown onion in butter and 1 tablespoon olive oil. Once onion is slightly brown, add the garlic and back meat.

Add the chicken stock and water and bring to a boil. Add the ham hock, seasoning, salt, jalapeños and liquid, and a drizzle of olive oil. Cover and reduce the heat to medium. Cook for about 1 hour, stirring occasionally.

While the stock is simmering, wash the collard greens thoroughly. Remove the thicker part of the stem or rib, literally tearing the leafy part off the rib and keeping some of the thinner rib for cooking. (The thicker rib is very bitter.)

Stack 6 to 8 leaves on top of each other and roll them "cigar style"; slice the rolled stack into ½- to 1-inch ribbons. Repeat with remaining leaves until all have been ribboned. Add the collard ribbons to the stockpot with meat, stirring occasionally, and cook until the greens are tender, about 45 minutes to 1 hour. Adjust seasonings to taste.

To make the wonton filler, remove the collard greens from the pot with a slotted spoon—allowing as much juice as possible to drain—and transfer to a large mixing bowl. Remove ham hock and back meat and chop into small pieces. Place the chopped meat into the bowl with the collard greens.

Mix the softened cream cheese into the meat and collards, folding first and then working it into the mixture.

Lay out a row of the wontons on a work surface and have a small bowl of water handy. Dip your finger into the water and run wet finger along the four sides of each wonton wrapper. Place a scant teaspoon of collards mixture in the center of each and fold into a triangle. Set on a parchment-lined baking sheet and cover with a damp paper towel or cheesecloth until ready to fry. Repeat for the remaining wrappers.

Heat 3 or so inches of peanut oil (canola or Crisco if there are peanut allergies) in a heavy-bottomed deep pot to 350 degrees.

Fry the wontons in batches of 7 to 10 until they are golden brown, about 3 to 4 minutes per batch. Place on paper towels to drain, and allow wontons to cool for 5 minutes before serving. They taste fantastic hot or at room temperature.

Farmer's Note: Sheets of phyllo dough can be used in place of wonton wrappers and thus baked rather than fried. Assemble in the same fashion, layering the dough and folding into triangles. Brush with oil or an egg wash and bake at 350 degrees for 12 to 15 minutes, until golden brown.

*Back meat is a very meaty pork chop that I like to cook with my collards. It cooks down to a very tender piece of meat and is delicious in these greens. The ham hock adds a salty, smoky flavor.

**You can adjust the amount of jalapeño up or down to suit your heat threshold.

WASHING COLLARDS

As newlyweds, my grandparents lived in Japan during their honeymoon years. Upon return to the States for seminary, my grandparents bought a washing machine. This was a pretty spectacular purchase for a seminary student and his young bride, but with three babies under the age of two, many diapers and clothes were in need of washing!

Mimi was gifted a bushel of collards by a local farmer. She knew that such a gift was precious in its own right and so she set about washing the bushel of collards—a significant amount of greens. A bushel of collard greens can feed a mess load of folks!

Sand and silt needed to be washed from the leaves and ribs of the collard greens, and three babies also needed her attention. So Mimi put her new washing machine to use—multitasking at its finest! Collards are not meant to be washed in a washing machine regardless of the cycle!

A clogged machine and ruined collards ensued. So whenever she prepared collard greens from that point forward, she always made sure to hand wash them—no matter how long it took or how many babies were crying!

Pork Tenderloin with Teriyaki Apricot Sauce

Serves 4–6

Grilling pork tenderloin is quite a marvelous method for preparing this meat. I use oak wood specifically for the flavor of its smoke.

1 pound pork tenderloin	Salt and pepper
Olive oil	Teriyaki Apricot Sauce (see below)

Pat the tenderloin dry with paper towels. Lightly baste the meat with olive oil, then rub on salt and pepper to taste.

Grill over medium for about 12 to 15 minutes, turning every 1 to 2 minutes, until a thermometer shows the inside temperature of the meat has reached about 145 to 150 degrees. Remove meat from the grill and tent or wrap it in foil. It will continue to cook and may even reach "well done" at 160 to 165 degrees.

Slice and serve with Teriyaki Apricot Sauce.

TERIYAKI APRICOT SAUCE

1 cup apricot preserves	1 teaspoon minced garlic
½ cup teriyaki sauce	Pinch of salt and pepper
¼ cup soy sauce	3 drops liquid smoke
1 teaspoon dark sesame oil	Olive oil, optional
1 teaspoon minced fresh gingerroot	

Warm the preserves and vigorously whisk together all ingredients except olive oil, which may be used to thin the sauce if needed. Excellent with pork, chicken, fish and shrimp.

Summer Salad with Goat Cheese and Berries

Serves 4

If you need to feed a great host of folks, plan on about 1 cup of leafy greens per person and ¼ cup or more per person of the fruity add-ons. Allow 4 to 6 ounces crumbled goat cheese per four people. You can always use leftover salad ingredients in other recipes.

4 cups salad greens of your choice (e.g., spring greens, spinach, Bibb lettuce, red leaf lettuce, radicchio, etc.)	1 cup Mandarin orange segments, drained
1 cup sliced strawberries	4–6 ounces goat cheese, crumbled
	Raspberry Balsamic Vinaigrette (see below)

Toss salad greens and serve in a large bowl. Offer fruity add-ons in smaller dishes. The vinaigrette can be served in a pretty dish, a gravy boat with a ladle, or a Mason jar.

RASPBERRY BALSAMIC VINAIGRETTE

Makes about 2 cups

1 cup olive, salad or pecan oil	1 teaspoon lemon juice
2 tablespoons raspberry preserves, heated slightly	½ teaspoon lemon zest
½ cup fresh raspberries, muddled with a scant amount of sugar	⅓ cup good-quality balsamic vinegar
	½ teaspoon salt
	½ teaspoon pepper

Whisk, blend, or shake all ingredients together—whatever strikes your fancy—and serve with the salad. This vinaigrette also makes a fine marinade for chicken, fish, or pork, or can be reduced as a sauce for meats.

Grits with Assorted Toppings

Serves 100

A five-pound bag of grits will serve 100 guests. If not serving a multitude, then follow the instructions on the grits package. Stone-ground grits are courser and may require more liquid. You can always add more milk, but it's the water to grits ratio at the beginning that is key. *Always* salt your boiling water. Grits will absorb the salt while cooking. As Mimi taught me, "Salt is an ingredient when making grits, not a condiment."

3	gallons water	2	(5-pound) bags grits
¼	cup salt	1	pound butter
¼	cup pepper	8	ounces (1 block) cream cheese, optional
1	gallon whole milk	4	cups shredded cheese, optional

Bring water to a boil and add the salt and pepper.

Add the milk and stir. Add the grits and whisk often.

Cook on low heat for almost 1 hour, continuing to whisk often.

Once grits have thickened, add the butter and stir to melt and incorporate it.

Farmer's Note: To make cheese grits, add one block of cream cheese and 4 cups of shredded cheddar for ultra creamy and cheesy style grits. Pepper Jack or pimento cheese (about 6 cups, respectively) also makes wonderful cheese grits.

TOPPINGS FOR GRITS:

Crumbled sausage	Shredded cheddar cheese
Cubed ham	Mozzarella balls or shredded mozzarella
Crumbled bacon	
Chopped green pepper	Sour cream
Pickled jalapeño	Sliced mushrooms
Browned garlic	Pickled okra
Chopped tomato	Baby shrimp
Chopped onion	Smoked salts

Fried Green Tomatoes

Serves 4–6

Growing up, I wondered why we Southerners would waste an unripe 'mater, for the flavor is achieved upon ripening, right? Well, in the case of tomatoes, the answer is twofold.

First off, a green tomato is spicy and full of expected tomato flavor. A ripened tomato is simply the intensified version of this flavor. Yet the green stage retains a heat that the red or ripened stage does not. A green tomato has a flavor that I like in pastas or for pickling.

Now, we Southerners love any excuse to fry something, and my theory is thus about frying green tomatoes: a ripe 'mater will just fall apart! But green ones are firm and will fry beautifully and hold up to dunking into a rémoulade, Mimi's Mustard Sauce or mayo. Plus, it is inevitable that a green tomato will get knocked off the vine or mistakenly picked before ripening, so consumption must be de rigueur.

As a gardener, I am overwhelmed each season with the plethora a plot will produce. The first and last tomatoes off the vine will be green and must be used. Trust me, tomatoes—as with squash, zucchini, okra and peppers—will keep on producing if tended. There are umpteen ways to use a red or ripened tomato; we might as well give the green tomato its time to shine!

6 medium-size green tomatoes

4 cups House-Autry breading mix, divided

1½ cups water

3 tablespoons buttermilk

Salt and pepper

6 cups oil for frying, divided

Wash and slice the tomatoes into ¼- to ½-inch slices.

Heat 4 cups oil to 350 to 375 degrees in a cast-iron skillet.

Meanwhile, pour 2 cups House-Autry breading mix onto a rimmed plate. In a medium-size bowl, combine the remaining 2 cups breading mix with water and buttermilk, and then bathe the tomatoes in the wet mixture. Dip each slice of coated tomato into the dry breading.

Fry breaded tomatoes in batches until golden brown, about 2 minutes per side. If the oil becomes depleted or becomes too cloudy, add the remaining 2 cups oil to the pan and wait while it heats up to temperature. Set fried tomatoes on paper towels to drain.

Serve with your favorite sauce, such as a rémoulade, Mimi's Mustard Sauce (see page 100), Mere's Tartar Sauce (see page 153) or a Vidalia sauce (see page 155).

Farmer's Note: if House-Autry is not available in your neck of the woods, a blend of all-purpose flour, cornmeal, seasoned salt, garlic salt, red pepper and onion powder can be substituted.

Also, grilled or poached shrimp and crab salad are perfect complements to fried green tomatoes!

Peach Cobbler

Serves 4–6

If there is one peach cobbler recipe, there are a thousand. You can make cobblers in iron skillets or baking dishes, and there is hardly anything better in the peach days of summer. Cobblers are "cuppa, cuppa, cuppa" dishes, whereas roughly a cup of (ergo, "cuppa") a few ingredients make up the dish. Rather than a groom's cake, Brince opted for a cobbler bar—stocked with ice cream, whipped cream, and his favorite cobbler!

Cuppa butter (1 stick)

Cuppa or two peaches (4–6 peaches, peeled and sliced)

1 tablespoon vanilla

Cuppa or so Bisquick (1½ cups)

Cuppa sugar (1 scant cup if peaches are sweet)

Cuppa milk (1 cup)

Almost cuppa buttermilk (½ cup)

Cuppa ice cream on top a cuppa cobbler!

Preheat oven to 350 degrees.

Melt butter in a 9 x 13-inch baking dish and add peaches to the hot butter (this fries them a tad). Add vanilla, too, and mix together.

Combine Bisquick, sugar and milks and pour over buttered peaches.

Bake for 45 minutes, or until golden brown. Serve with ice cream.

RESOURCES

PLANTS

Blooming Colors
1192 South Donahue St
Auburn, Alabama 36830
334.821.7929
bloomingcolors.net

BONNIE PLANTS
bonnieplants.com

THE GROWERS EXCHANGE
11110 Sandy Fields Rd
Richmond, VA 23030
1.888.829.6201
thegrowers-exchange.com

MONROVIA GROWERS
monrovia.com

MILLSTONE MARKET
6993 Poplar Avenue
Germantown, TN 38138
901.503.4711
triciasmillstone.com

PETALS FROM THE PAST
16034 County Rd 29
Jemison, AL 35085
205.646.0069
petalsfromthepast.com

SOUTHERN GROWERS
3601 Wetumpka Highway
Montgomery, AL 36110
1.800.627.1387 / 334.272.2140
southerngrowers.com

SOUTHERN HOMES AND GARDENS

8820 Vaughn Rd
Montgomery, AL 36117
334.387.0440
southernhomesandgardens.com

ANTIQUES, ACCENTS AND ACCOUTREMENTS

Sometimes, you just never know what you'll find at an antique show, market, or store. I love perusing for linens, tableware and silver at these haunts—and maybe a table and sideboard too.

ANTIQUES AND BEYOND
1853 Cheshire Bridge Rd NE
Atlanta, GA 30324-4923
404.872.4342
antiquesandbeyond.com

BECKETT ANTIQUES AND
COTTAGE COLLECTION AND
ASHLEY GILBREATH/PARISH
514 Cloverdale Rd,
   Suites C, D and E
Montgomery, AL 36106
rebeccacumbieantiques.com
cottagecollectionsantiques.com
ashleygilbreath.com

BOXWOODS GARDENS AND GIFTS

100 E Andrews Dr NW
Atlanta, GA 30305-1315
404.233.3400
boxwoodsonline.com

DOVETAIL ANTIQUES
252 Hwy 107 S
Cashiers, NC 28717
828.743.1800

FOXGLOVE ANTIQUES
699 Miami Circle
Atlanta, GA 30324
404.233.0222
foxgloveantiques.com

FRANCIE HARGROVE
95 Hwy 107 S
Cashiers, NC 28717
828.743.9700
franciehargrove.com

HEERY'S TOO
184 E. Clayton St
Athens, GA 30601
706.552.3886
heerystoo.com

INITIAL REACTION
906 Carroll St
Perry, GA 31069
478.224.2425
Monogramming

JAMES FARMER INC.
936 Carroll St
Perry, GA 31069

LE CREUSET
lecreuset.com

LODGE CAST IRON
lodgemfg.com

MAGGIE GRIFFIN
INTERIOR DESIGN
bellissimoandbella.blogspot.com
Custom menu painting,
interiors and events

ONWARD RESERVE
146 E Clayton St
Athens, GA 30601
706.543.0106

3089 Peachtree Rd NE
Atlanta, GA 30305
404.814.8997
onwardreserve.com

PEACHTREE BATTLE
ANTIQUES
2395 Peachtree Rd, NE
Atlanta, GA 30305-4147
404.846.9411
peachtreebattleantiques.com

PLACE ON THE POINTE
2416 Westgate Dr, Ste A
Albany, GA 31707
229.883.8585

PROVVISTA DESIGNS
provvistadesigns.com
(all basket-weave, cream and white
dinnerware throughout the book)

SCOTT'S ANTIQUE MARKET
Atlanta Expo Center
3650 and 3850 Jonesboro Rd
Atlanta, GA 30354
404.361.2000
Second weekend of every month

STAR PROVISIONS
1198 Howell Mill Rd
Atlanta, GA 30318
404.365.0410
starprovisions.com

THE SALT TABLE
51 Barnard St
Savannah, GA 31401
912.447.0200
salttable.com

TABLE MATTERS
2402 Montevallo Rd
Birmingham, AL 35223
205.879.0125
table-matters.com

THE WHITE CRANE
1407 Monte Sano Ave
Augusta, GA 30904
706.738.6359
thewhitecrane.com

DINNERWARE PROVIDED
THROUGH:
provvistadesigns.com

FARMS AND MARKETS
AND CATERERS
Anson Mills
1922 C Gervais St
Columbia, SC 29201
803.467.4122
ansonmills.com

BELLE CHEVRE
18849 Upper Fort Hampton Rd
Elkmont, AL 35620
256.732.3577
bellechevre.com

BJ SMITH EVENTS
AND CATERING
Tifton, GA
229.392.2913

BUTTERMILK PIE COMPANY
Amanda Willbanks
302 Broad St SE, Ste C
Gainesville, GA 30501
706.499.5234
buttermilkpieco.com

CASHIERS FARMERS
MARKET
78 Hwy 64 E
Cashiers, NC 28717
828.743.4334
cashiersfarmersmarket.com

CENTRAL MARKET
centralmarket.com

COUSIN'S CATERING
Leon Holloway
Americus, GA
229.924.6846

DAPHNE LODGE
2502 U.S. 280
Cordele, GA 31015
229.273.2596
daphnelodge.com

THE DRUGSTORE DELI AND
SARA JO MCLEAN CATERING
100 E Heritage Blvd
Byron, GA 31008
478.654.6037

ELLIS BROTHERS PECANS
1315 Tippettville Rd
Vienna, GA 31092-6213
229.268.9041
werenuts.com

EPTING EVENTS
1430 N. Chase St
Athens, GA 30601
706.353.1913
eptingevents.com

FIRE AND FLAVOR
1.866.728.8332
fireandflavor.com

GEORGIA OLIVE FARMS
229.482.3505
georgiaolivefarms.com

LANE SOUTHERN
ORCHARDS
50 Lane Rd
Fort Valley, GA 31030
800.27PEACH
lanesouthernorchards.com

LUCY'S MARKET
102 West Paces Ferry
   Rd, Ste 102-F
Atlanta, GA 30305
404.869.9222
lucysmarket.com

M AND T MEATS
230 Lower River Rd
Hawkinsville, GA 31036
478.892.9810
mtmeatco.com

MONTGOMERY
CURB MARKET
1004 Madison Ave
Montgomery, AL
334.263.6445
montgomeryal.gov

NORA MILL GRANARY
7107 S Main St
Helen, GA 30545
706.878.2375
noramill.com

PARTIES TO DIE FOR
partiestodieforatlanta.com

PEARSON FARM
5575 Zenith Mill Rd
Zenith, Crawford, GA 31030
478.827.0750
pearsonfarm.com

THE PERFECT PEAR
922 Carroll St
Perry, GA 31069

STRIPLING'S GENERAL STORE
2289 GA Hwy 300 S
Cordele, GA 31015
striplings.com

THE SWANSON
933 Carroll St.
Perry, GA 31069
478.987.1938
theswanson.com

SWEET GRASS DAIRY
106 N Broad St
Thomasville, GA 31792
229.228.6704
sweetgrassdairy.com

TWIN OAKS FARM
twinoaksfarmweddings.com

WHITE OAK PASTURES
22775 Highway 27
Bluffton, GA 39824
229.641.2081
whiteoakpastures.com

WILLIAM L. BROWN FARMS
AKA FARMER BROWN'S
4334 Highway 49 North
Montezuma, GA 31063
478.472.8767
williamlbrownfarms.com

YOUR STATE FARMERS
MARKETS AND LOCAL
FARM STANDS

SUBSTITUTIONS

1 cup self-rising flour	1 cup all-purpose flour plus 1 teaspoon baking powder and ½ teaspoon salt
1 cup cake flour	1 cup all-purpose flour minus 2 tablespoons
1 tablespoon flour (as thickener)	½ tablespoon cornstarch or ½ tablespoon potato starch or ½ tablespoon arrowroot starch 1 tablespoon quick-cooking tapioca
I cup commercial sour cream	1 tablespoon lemon juice or vinegar plus evaporated milk to make 1 cup or 3 tablespoons butter plus ⅞ cup sour milk
1 cup yogurt	1 cup buttermilk or sour cream
1 cup sour milk or buttermilk	1 tablespoon lemon juice or vinegar plus sweet milk to make 1 cup
1 cup whole milk	1 cup reconstituted nonfat milk plus 2½ teaspoons butter or ½ cup evaporated milk plus ½ cup water
1 cup light cream (for cooking only)	3 tablespoons butter plus ⅞ cup milk
1 cup heavy cream	⅓ cup butter plus ¾ cup milk
1 cup corn syrup	1 cup sugar plus ¼ cup liquid called for in recipe
1 cup honey	1¼ cups sugar plus ¼ cup water
1 ounce unsweetened chocolate	3 tablespoons cocoa plus 1 tablespoon butter
1 clove fresh garlic	1 teaspoon garlic salt or ⅛ teaspoon garlic powder
1 teaspoon onion powder	2 teaspoons minced onion
1 tablespoon fresh herbs	1 teaspoon ground or crushed dry herbs
1 pound fresh mushrooms	6 ounces canned mushrooms
1 teaspoon dry mustard	I tablespoon prepared mustard
¼ cup chopped fresh parsley	1 tablespoon dry parsley

This list is influenced by many a good ol' Southern cookbook whose recipes and
substitutions alike have been inspired and flavored my cooking.

ACKNOWLEDGMENTS

It takes a village to raise a child, and I am proof of such raising! Thank you to all who have helped cook, prepare, photograph and simply support me in this venture. I am thankful to have you in my village!

Thank you, Paula and Mark Hennessey, Francie and Shannon Hargrove, Linda and Darwin James, Aunt Kathy and Uncle Gerry, Aunt Gari Griffin, Twin Oaks Farm (Karen and Tom Hunt), Joni and Randy Coody, Lyn and Bob McLeod, Sara Jo McLean, Susie Williams, Brenda and Albert Simon, Maggie Griffin, Nancy and Charlie Golsen and hosts of others. I cannot thank you enough!

To my fabulous photographers: there is nothing like working with your sister and a dear friend. Thank you, Maggie and Emily!

To my amazing staff: y'all are the backbone of James Farmer Inc! Stacey Byrd, Laura Lyn Coody, Jason Ponegalek and Sami Stimus—thank you for keeping JFI and James Farmer, for that matter, on the go!

Thank you, Granddaddy, Mama, Daddy and Julie, Maggie and Zach and Napp, Meredith and Sampson, and Aunt Kathy and Uncle Gerry for always being my biggest help, support and heartbeat! Love y'all!

PHOTO CREDITS

Ashlee Culverhouse: pages 158–63, 166–75
Emily Followill: pages 6, 8, 42–55, 76–89, 122–57
Maggie Yelton: pages 2, 4, 10–41, 56–75, 90–121, 164, 178–86, 190–96
Vue Photography: page 187

INDEX OF RECIPES

Metric Conversion Chart

VOLUME MEASUREMENTS		WEIGHT MEASUREMENTS		TEMPERATURE CONVERSION	
U.S.	METRIC	U.S.	METRIC	FAHRENHEIT	CELSIUS
1 teaspoon	5 ml	$\frac{1}{2}$ ounce	15 g	250	120
1 tablespoon	15 ml	1 ounce	30 g	300	150
$\frac{1}{4}$ cup	60 ml	3 ounces	90 g	325	160
$\frac{1}{3}$ cup	75 ml	4 ounces	115 g	350	180
$\frac{1}{2}$ cup	125 ml	8 ounces	225 g	375	190
$\frac{2}{3}$ cup	150 ml	12 ounces	350 g	400	200
$\frac{3}{4}$ cup	175 ml	1 pound	450 g	425	220
1 cup	250 ml	$2\frac{1}{4}$ pounds	1 kg	450	230

Summer Picnic

Ants on a Log
Devilish Deviled Eggs
Goat Cheese Zucchini Roll-Ups
Caprese Panzanella
Pressed Picnic Sandwich
Pasta Salad à la Pepper
Cucumber & Radish Salad
Picnic Parfaits with Granola Crumble & Berries
Mini Brown Sugar Blueberry Pies

Rehearsal Dinner
on the grounds

Baked Chicken with Peach Glaze
Spinach Salad with Berries & Feta Cheese
& Honey-Lemon Vinaigrette
Pimento Cheese Mini Sandwiches
French Green Beans
Tortellini Salad with Artichokes, Tomatoes & Olives
Cucumber Sandwiches
Gazpacho Shooters
Watermelon Ice
Sour Cream Biscuits
Orange Sorbet with Baboo's Tea
Mama Doris's Banana Pudding with ___

Family Reunion

-LUNCH-
Strawberry-Almond Spinach Salad with Poppyseed Dressing
Asian-Style Chicken Salad with Sesame Dressing
Basil-Caper Shrimp Salad
Corn & Onion Salad
Feta and Olive Pasta Salad
Potato Salad
Herb & Poppyseed Rolls
Jalapeño Corn Muffins
Peach Buttermilk Pound Cake
Chocolate-Glazed Chocolate Pound Cake
-DINNER-
Fried Chicken
Sweet-and-Sour Slaw
Gerry's World-Famous Baked Beans
Mema's Macaroni & Cheese
Deluxe Mac 'n' Cheese
Ribs with Steamer's Sauce

JTF

Barn Dinner
in the Mountains

Basil Blackberry Salad with Goat Cheese

Baked Tomato "Twists" with Honey

Cashiers Farmers Market Pasta

Garlicky Wilted Kale

Toasted Pound Cake
with Plums, Peaches &
Strawberry Sauce

JTF

Birthday Dinner
in Highlands

Roasted Medley of Potatoes & O...

Dilly-Creamed Corn Cornbread

Brie and Cucumber Salad with

Sautéed Summer Peas

Bacon-Wrapped Pork Tenderloin

Grown-Up Dirt Cake

Mayhaw Dress...

Fireside Dinne
on the Mountain

Oven-Poached Salmon

Sweet Potato Wedges with

Roasted Okra

Skillet Toast

Roasted Squash & Zucchini

Honey-Lemon Olive Oil Cake

Rosemary Butter

Amaretto Peach Bake